I0191293

FIFTH ANNUAL CONFERENCE

OF THE

YOUNG PEOPLE'S SOCIETIES

OF

CHRISTIAN ENDEAVOR CONVENTION

HELD AT

SARATOGA SPRINGS, NEW

YORK.

July 6 - 8, 1886.

First Fruits Press
Wilmore, Kentucky
c2015

First Fruits Press
The Academic Open Press of Asbury Theological Seminary
204 N. Lexington Ave., Wilmore, KY 40390
859-858-2236
first.fruits@asburyseminary.edu
asbury.to/firstfruits

FIFTH ANNUAL CONFERENCE

OF THE

YOUNG PEOPLE'S SOCIETY

OF

CHRISTIAN ENDEAVOR,

HELD AT SARATOGA SPRINGS, NEW YORK,

JULY 6, 7 AND 8, 1886.

PRINTERS 230 LEWIS & WINSHIP HIGH ST. LYNN, MASS.

PREFACE.

In locating the Fifth Annual Conference of the Y. P. S. of C. E. at Saratoga, the Executive Committee were influenced by the fact that the work had spread so widely during the past year that it was no longer fair to a large constituency to ask of them to come so far east as the localities where the earlier conferences had been held. Saratoga seemed to be about a central point, as nearly as could be judged. Saratoga, too, was easily reached from all quarters, while, through its almost innumerable hotels and boarding-houses, it offered accommodations for delegates not to be obtained elsewhere. Still, it was with some hesitancy that it was finally decided to hold the conference outside of New England. A wiser hand than theirs guided the Executive Committee in their deliberations, and the success of the conference which has just closed has proved the wisdom of His choice. It had been felt that the enthusiasm and the encouragement attendant upon a large gathering were essential to obtaining the best results from such a meeting. Should we, outside of New England, have an attendance which would guarantee these features? You who were present at Saratoga know how that question was answered. The meetings were held in the Washington Street Methodist Church, that great building erected largely for the conferences of such great bodies as the American Board of Foreign Missions, and all through the meetings of those three days the body of the house was filled with an interested, attentive and enthusiastic audience. Certainly God was very good to us during that convention, and by showing, as we believe, his approval of the cause, has placed the Society of Christian Endeavor in a prominent position among the ranks of the organizations which have for an aim the evangelization of the world.

In publishing this report, it is hoped to accomplish a twofold object; first, to furnish to those who were present at the meetings a reminder of all that was said and done on that occasion, and, secondly, to give to the many who were unable to be present some of the benefits so plentifully gained by those who were in attendance, that all may partake of the blessings. The report is not as complete as we could wish. Several important and valuable addresses it has been impossible to obtain, either from the fact that they were never committed to paper, or from some other equally good reason. Still, in the main it is correct, and we send it forth with the hope that God, in His goodness and wisdom, will guide this little book where it will carry to its readers, some of the many blessings, the cause of Christian Endeavor has so generously bestowed on at least fifty thousand young people of this and other lands.

GEO. M. WARD,

General Secretary.

MINUTES.

The Fifth Annual Conference of the Young People's Society of Christian Endeavor was held in the Washington Street Methodist Church of Saratoga Springs, N. Y., on Tuesday, Wednesday and Thursday, July 6th, 7th and 8th, 1886.

The Conference opened at 5 P. M. on Tuesday with a meeting for organization and business, President Van Patten in the chair. After devotional exercises, led by Rev. H. B. Grose of Poughkeepsie, N. Y., and Rev. J. C. Kerr of Elizabeth, N. J., the conference proceeded at once to the transaction of the necessary business.

On motion of Rev. R. W. Brokaw of Belleville, N. J., A. L. Winship of Lynn, Mass., was chosen scribe of the conference. On motion of Rev. F. E. Clark of South Boston, a committee on credentials was appointed by the chair, consisting of Messrs. Baldwin of Manchester, N. H., Hazeltine of South Boston, Mass., Williams of Freeport, Me., Noble of Weeping Water, Nebraska, Hamilton of Elizabeth, N. J., Dean of Poughkeepsie, N. Y., Everett of Jamesburg, N. Y.

On motion of Mr. Pennell of Portland, Me., the President was instructed to bring in a list of committees for the conference, and to select members for the same. In accordance with the above motion, President Van Patten announced as the Business Committee: Secretary George M. Ward of Boston, Mass., Chairman; Mr. Eli Manchester of New Haven, Conn., Mr. J. T. Alling of Rochester, N. Y. The appointment of the remaining committees was postponed till the following day.

Rev. Mr. Dickinson of Lowell, Mass., then presented resolutions, as follows:

> In view of the fact that the Society of Christian Endeavor is organized to promote certain definite and specified ends of Christian nurture, and that its provisions for appointing special committees in the local society are such as to give the broadest scope for every form of philanthropy and Christian work,
>
> Resolved, That a special committee of three be appointed by the President at the opening of the session, to which all resolutions, memorials and propositions shall be handed on or before the second day of the session of the convention, each resolution to contain the name of the proposer and the name of the association he represents, these resolutions, etc., to be at once referred to the committee without reading.

After hearty endorsement from Messrs. Clark, Brokaw and others, these resolutions were adopted by the conference.

An assignment of rooms was then made by Secretary Ward, to be used during this conference by the various committees.

At six o'clock the meeting adjourned till evening.

5

EVENING SESSION.

At seven thirty the conference was again in session. After reading of scripture, prayer by Rev. Mr. Spears, of Middlebury, Vt., and singing by the congregation, led by a choir selected from the various delegates, Rev. C. F. Deems, D. D. L. L. D., of the church of the Strangers, New York city, preached a most able and instructive sermon, taking his text from II. Kings, 6:17: "And Elisha prayed, and the Lord opened the eyes of the young man and he saw." At the close of the sermon a solo was very finely rendered by Miss Jennie Vorn Holz, of Lowell, Mass. After announcement from the committee on credentials and singing by the congregation, the benediction was pronounced by Dr. Deems.

WEDNESDAY FORENOON.

At 9 A. M., the conference resumed its session. After a brief prayer-meeting, led by Rev. T. W. Jones of Saratoga, in which the results of a Christian Endeavor training were brought plainly to the front, the conference proceeded to the regular business of the day.

The Business Committee, through its chairman, Mr. Ward, announced the programme for the day. President Van Patten then reported the following committees :

Nominating Committee—Rev. S. W. Adriance of Lowell, Mass., Chairman ; Mr. W. H. Childs of North Manchester, Conn., Mr. F. K. Adams of Rochester, N. Y., Mr. C. B. Holdrege of Bloomington, Ill., Mr. I. S. Colwell of Syracuse, N. Y.

Committee on Resolutions—Rev. C. A. Dickinson, Lowell, Mass., Chairman ; Rev. J. C. Kerr, Elizabeth, N. J., Mr. W. H. Pennell, Portland, Me., Mr. S. D. Hodges, Burlington, Vt., Mr. H. M. Kaisinger, Hatboro, Pa.

Finance Committee—Rev. J. L. Hill, Lynn, Mass., Chairman ; Mr. Choate Burnham, South Boston, Mass.. Mr. A. W. Burnham, Lowell, Mass.

Next followed the report of the General Secretary, George M. Ward, which is printed in full in the Appendix. The report was accepted, and, on motion of Rev. Mr. Brokaw, was referred to a committee consisting of Rev. Mr. Brokaw, Belleville, N. J., Mr. Hodgkins, St. Albans, Vt., Mr. Visscher, Springfield, Ohio, Mr. Morgan, St. Louis, Mo., Mr. Parsons, Oneida, N. Y.

The report of the Treasurer, Wm. Shaw of South Boston, was next read, followed by some very able suggestions on the financial problem. Mr. Shaw advocated the use of the pledge cards in the society. The report and suggestions were referred to the Finance Committee.

Then followed the reading of the President's address, which, together with the other papers, may be found in the Appendix. The address was referred to a special committee consisting of Rev. Mr. Clark, South Boston, Mass., Rev. Mr. Boynton, Haverhill, Mass., Rev. Mr. Grose, Poughkeepsie, N. Y., Rev. Mr. Fiske, Bethel, Vt., Mr. Graham, New York city.

The roll of members in the United Society of Christian Endeavor was then called, and a meeting of the corporation, to be held in the vestry, was announced.

Vice-President Rev. Erastus Blakeslee of New Haven was then called to the chair, and two minute " reports from the work " were called for.

Rev. Mr. Mills of Newburyport was the first speaker. He referred especially to the good accomplished among the young ladies of his congregation, and the general advance of the work.

W. H. Childs of North Manchester, Ct., responded to a call for a report from that place. The advance has been great; the membership of the union, which was organized a year ago, is rapidly increasing; a large number of Endeavor societies are being rapidly formed, and a majority of the young people who join the church are members of the societies.

Mr. Boynton of Rye, N. H., said that societies had been formed in his locality which were rapidly increasing in membership. His state did not have as many societies as Maine or Connecticut, but they were growing in numbers.

Mrs. Slocum of Gilman, Iowa, reported for several societies in her vicinity. She gave an account of her work among the children of " outside families," who were unaccustomed to attend church. She started with one or two, and the number has gradually increased until quite a large attendance has been secured. Her report was very interesting, and claimed the attention of all present.

Brief reports followed from Messrs. Adams of Rochester, N. Y., Pitkin of Palmyra, N. Y., Hill of Syracuse, N. Y., Arns of Sunderland, Mass., Hamilton of Elizabeth, N. J., Benedict of Kensington, Conn., Kaisinger of Hatboro, Pa., Stevens of Providence, R. I., Bloomfield of Pawtucket, R. I., Bennett of Cambridge, Mass., Pond of Franklin, Mass., and Mrs. Lathe of Northampton, Mass.

All of the above reports presented most encouraging features. Among the most interesting was the report from Syracuse, N. Y., where the membership of the Sunday school had been increased from 175 to 327 through the efforts of the Y. P. S. C. E.

Rev. Erastus Blakeslee then reported for the Connecticut State organization. His report will be found, with the other papers of the conference, in the Appendix.

Mr. Pennell, for the Trustees, reported the following list of officers elected at the corporate meeting of the U. S. C. E.: Chairman, W. J. Van Patten; Clerk, W. H. Pennell; Treasurer, Wm. Shaw; Auditor, A. W. Burnham; Trustees, four years, Rev. N. Boynton and Choate Burnham.

Dr. Deems of New York followed this report with a few words of encouragement and good cheer, and closed the morning session with the benediction.

WEDNESDAY AFTERNOON.

The afternoon session was opened with prayer by Rev. Mr. Brokaw and singing by congregation.

The first paper of the afternoon was that of Rev. C. P. Mills of Newburyport, Mass., on "The Use of Hymn Singing in These Meetings." Following this paper, which is printed in the Appendix, the suggestion was offered that a committee be appointed to look into the matter of arranging a collection of songs for the Y. P. S. C. E., and report to the Sixth Annual Conference.

Copies of the following hymn, written for the Y. P. S. C. E., by Rev. J. E. Rankin, D. D., were then distributed through the audience and all joined in singing " Our National Hymn":

KEEP YOUR COLORS FLYING.
By Rev. J. E. Rankin, D. D.

1. Keep your colors flying,
    All ye Christian youth;
    To Christ's call replying,
    Full of grace and truth.
    Rise in strength and beauty,
    In life's morning glow,
    Answer to each duty,
    Onward, upward go.

CHORUS: Keep your colors flying,
            Stand for God and truth;
         Keep your colors flying,
            All ye Christian youth.

2. Life is all before you
    Where to choose your way;
    Keep Christ's colors o'er you,
    Watch and fight and pray.
    With a firm endeavor
    Every foe defy;
    True to Jesus ever,
    Lift your colors high.

3. Keep your colors flying,
    Never think of ease;
    Sin and self denying,
    Jesus only please.
    Not for worldly pleasure,
    Not for worldly fame,
    Not for heaps of treasure;
    Live for Jesus' name.

On motion of Rev. Mr. Boynton, Mr. Mill's paper was referred to the executive committee. At this point the President called for the report of the Finance Committee. Rev. Mr. Hill, the chairman, set forth in a clear and concise manner the exact condition of affairs and made plain the need of funds. After an eloquent statement of the great good which might be done in the future, could the funds requisite be obtained, he gave to those present an opportunity to aid in the work. The response was immediate and generous: for the next hour the work of raising the funds was continued until the handsome sum of $2,028 was reached. The following is a list of the subscriptions made both personal and from societies, together with a list of those persons who were made life members:

Rev. Mr. Mills, Newburyport, Mass.,	$ 5 00
Park Place Ch., Pawtucket, R. I.,	5 00
First Presbyterian, Palmyra, N. Y.,	5 00
Phillips Church, So. Boston,	50 00
Winthrop Ch., Charleston, Mass.,	15 00
Central Presbyterian, Rochester, N. Y.,	50 00
Oneida, N. Y.,	25 00
North Presbyterian, Rochester, N. Y.,	15 00
Tabernacle, Jersey City.	15 00
Children's, So. Gilman, Iowa,	5 00
Cash.	1 00
Mr. Hunter. North Adams, Mass.,	5 00
First Congregational, Springfield, Ohio,	10 00
Rev. Mr. Boynton, Rye, N. H.,	5 00
Hadley, Mass.,	5 00
First Baptist Ch., Syracuse, N. Y.,	10 00
First Presbyterian, Booneville, N. Y.,	5 00
" " Schnan, N. Y.,	5 00
Third " Elizabeth, N. J.,	10 00
Congregational, Manchester, Iowa.,	5 00
Cash	5 00
First Congregational, Burlington, Vt.,	25 00
North " Haverhill, Mass.,	60 00
West " " "	10 00
Y. P. S. C. E., Bethel. Vt.,	5 00
Third Congregational, Burlington, Vt.,	15 00
Reformed, Belleville, N. J.,	10 00
First Congregational, Milford, N. H.,	15 00
Congregational. Vergennes, Vt.	10 00
Second Congregational, West Newton, Mass.,	25 00
Presbyterian, Verona, N. Y.,	5 00
First Presbyterian, Booneville, N. Y.,	5 00
Second Congregational, Bridgeport, Conn.,	10 00
First " Wallingford, Conn.,	5 00
First Presbyterian, Easton, Pa.,	5 00
" " Jamesburg, N. J.,	5 00
Congregational, Melrose, Mass.,	15 00
Pilgrim Ch., St. Louis, Mo.,	25 00
Maple St., Danvers,	10 00
Baptist, Burlington, Vt.,	5 00
Williston, Portland, Me.,	25 00
St. Albans, for W. Hopkins,	20 00
Central, Fall River,	10 00
Kennebunk, Me.,	5 00
First Congregational, Lowell, Mass.,	10 00
Congregational, Ashfield, Mass ,	5 00
First Congregational, So. Egremont, Mass.,	10 00
" " Manchester, N. H.,	10 00
St. Timothy's, 57th St., New York	5 00
Second Congregational, Fair Haven, Conn.,	20 00
First Baptist, Meriden, Conn.,	5 00
First Congregational, Hyde Park,	15 00
Congregational, Middleburg, Vt.,	5 00
Eliot Ch., Lowell, Mass.,	25 00
North Avenue Congregational, Cambridge, Mass.,	25 00
Day St. Ch., Somerville,	5 00
Kirke St., Lowell, Mass.,	50 00
Cash,	1 00

Amount carried forward, $772 00

Amount brought forward,	$772 00
Church of Strangers, N. Y.,	15 00
North Church, Lynn, Mass,	40 00
Church, Grafton, Mass.,	20 00
First Congregational, St. Albans, Vt.,	25 00
First Congregational, Medina, Ohio,	10 00
Howard Avenue, New Haven, Conn,	10 00
Taylor,	5 00
Second Presbyterian, Bloomington, Ill.,	15 00
United Ch., New Haven, Conn.,	5 00
Congregational Ch., Central Falls, R. I.,	5 00
" " Northboro, Mass.,	5 00
Prospect St. Congregational, Newburyport, Mass.,	5 00
North Congregational, Newburyport, Mass.,	20 00
Presbyterian, Palmyra, N. Y.,	5 00
S. W. Adriance, Lowell, Mass.	5 00
Rev. Mr. Howard, West Medford, Mass.	5 00
Congregational Ch., Groton, Mass.	5 00
Second Parish, Portland, Me.	30 00
Congregational, Brandon, Vt.	5 00
Mystic, Medford, Mass.	10 00
North Pesbyterian, Rochester, N. Y.	10 00
First Congregational, North Hampton, Mass.	10 00
Second " " Manchester, Conn.	15 00
Swampscott, Mass.	5 00
First Baptist, Hatboro, Pa.	10 00
Woodfords, Me.	15 00
First Parish, Newburyport, Me.	5 00
Rollstone, Fitchburg, Mass.	16 00
Y. P. S. C. E., Conway, Mass.	10 00
First Baptist, Poughkeepsie, N. Y.	15 00
Congregational, Wellesley, Mass.	10 00
Central, Haverhill, Mass.	15 00
Congregational, Westford, Mass.	5 00
" Kennebunk, Me.	5 00
Kensington, Ct.	5 00
College St., Cambridge, Mass.	10 00
Y. P. S. C. E., West Haven	10 00
Westerly, R. I.	5 00
C. F. Stevens, Providence, R. I.	5 00
Miss Wilson, North Church, Lynn	5 00
First Church, Burlington, Vt.	15 00
Congregational church, Litchfield, Ct.	5 00
Fred Putnam, Booneville, Conn.	15 00
Society, Monroe, Ct.	3 00
J. L. Spicer, Society of Friends, Clark Corners, Saratoga	5 00
Litchfield, Mich.	5 00
United church, New Haven	5 00
Cash	5 00
Phillips church, So. Boston	25 00
Society, Shelburne Falls, Mass.	10 00
Cash	1 00
Y. P. S C. E., Gray, Me.	5 00
Miss S. Cecil	10 00
Y. P. S C. E., Littleton, Mass.	5 00
Jennie Cummings, Lynn	5 00
Cash, Mr Richmond	1 00
Mr. W. H. Parker, Lowell,	5 00
Amount carried forward,	$1,328 00

Amount brought forward,		$1,328 00
Second Congregational churcn, So. Windsor, Ct., ...		5 00
Sunderland church, Mass., ...		5 00
Mrs. Harry L. Cable, N. Y. City, ...		25 00
Congregational church, Newton. Iowa, ...		1 00
" " Cedar Rapids, Iowa.		1 00
M. E. Pond, Franklin, Md., ...		5 00
Reformed, Schenectady, N. Y., ...		10 00
First Congregational, Burlington, Vt., ...		10 00
Rev. F. E. Clark, (life member), ...		20 00
Dea. Burnham, So. Boston, ...		20 00
Rev. W. E. Strong, Beverly, ...		5 00
Rev. Mr. Boynton, for the "Boys,"		10 00
Foster, Winchendon, ...		5 00
C. A. Dickinson, (Mr. Hill), ...		20 00

Pennell. { H. B. Grose, Poughkeepsie, N. Y. 5 00
W. J. Van Patten 5 00
W. H. Wood, Burlington, Vt. 5 00
Rev. F. E. Clark 5 00

N. T. Dickinson, Glenville, N. Y., ... 5 00

Dickinson. { J. L. Sedgley, ... 5 00
J. L. Hill 5 00
Rev. Thwing 10 00

Mr. Stearns, Hadley . . . 2 00

Brokaw. { Rev. Earl, Fall River 5 00
First Cong., Walpole, Mass. 10 00
Y. P. S. C. E., Hartford, Vt. 5 00

Blakeslee. { Eli Manchester 5 00
A. H. Warner, Bridgeport, Conn. 5 00
Manchester, Conn , Society 10 00

Rev. Hawes. { Rev. N. K. Brown, Burlington, Vt. 20 00

Dr. Deems. { Church of Strangers, New York 5 00
Society, Clinton, Mass. 5 00
Society, Shelburne, Mass. 5 00
No. Amherst, Mass. 5 00

Addison P. Foster. { Tabernacle 5 00

First Congregational, Lowell, for Rev. Smith Baker 10 00

Amount carried forward,		$1,612 00

Amount brought forward,		$1,612 00
First Congregational, Springfield, Ohio, Rev. W. H. Ward		10 00
Society in North Manchester, Rev. H. W. Pope		5 00
Third Congregational, Burlington, Vt., Prof. Geo. H. Perkins		5 00
First Baptist, Poughkeepsie, Rev. H. B. Grose		5 00
First Congregational, Manchester, N. H., Rev. Sperry		10 00
Woodfords, Me., Pastor		5 00
Rev. Jones.	W. J. Van Patten	5 00
	Geo. M. Ward	5 00
	Mr. Willard	5 00
	C. H. Hermin, Randolph, Vt.	5 00
Society, Walpole, Mass., Rev. F. J. Marsh		10 00
Walnut Ave., Boston, Mass., Rev. A. H. Plumb		20 00
S. W. Adriance.	Wm. Shaw	5 00
	F. E. Clark	5 00
	Highland, Lowell	10 00
St. Albans, Rev. W. H. Hopkins		20 00
Central Church, Fall River, Rev. H. H. Earl		10 00
Eli Manchester.	Rev. Mr. Blakeslee	5 00
	College Street Society	5 00
	Howard Ave. Society	5 00
	Lillie Berwell	1 00
	J. H. Mansfield	2 00
	Mr. Perkins, Monroe	1 00
	Mr. Benedict, Kensington	1 00
Second Congregational, Bridgeport, Conn., Rev. Warner		10 00
Miss Alldredge.	Mr. Hill of Lynn	1 00
	C. J. Chase	1 00
	W. H. Childs, No. Manchester	1 00
	G. W. Griswold	1 00
	Rev. Brokaw	2 00
	Mr. F. K. Adams	1 00
	H. B. Grose	1 00
	Miss Manley	1 00
	Miss Vorn Holz	1 00
	Mr. Noble, Nebraska	1 00
	F. J. Shields	1 00
	Alice May	3 00
	Miss Gilmore	1 00
	Chas. T. Janes, Phillips Church	1 00
	Miss Anderson, Gray Church	1 00
W. R. Clark		1 00
Misses Partridge		2 00
Miss Manning		1 00
Mrs. Slocum.	Van Patten	2 00
	Howe, Upton, Mass.	1 00
	Mrs. Parker	1 00
	M. E. Pond	1 00
	Bessie Blakeslee	1 00
	Mrs. Jones, Saratoga	1 00
	Miss M. L. Nason	1 00
	Miss Williston, Kennebunk, Me.	1 00
	A. E. Fisher, Springfield	1 00

("Do Without Club.")

Amount carried forward,		$1,813 00

Amount brought forward,		$1,813 00
Mrs. Slocum.	Helen L. Rice	1 00
	W. H. Pennell	1 00
	Morgan, St. Louis	1 00
	Cash	1 00
	Geo. H. Allen	1 00
	Miss Fannie Lemon	1 00
	Parsons, Oneida	1 00
	M. A. Hudson	1 00
	Cash	1 00
	Cash	50
George F. Pitkin, for Rev. Warren H. Landon		10 00
Society in Advance, Palmyra, N. Y.		10 00
Rollstone, Fitchburg, Pastor		4 00
North Avenue, Cambridge, Mass., W. J. Mandell, E. F. Fobes		15 00
Misses Leach.	N. T. Brown	2 00
	West, Cornwall, Ct.	5 00
	Mrs. Hill	5 00
	Van Patten	3 00
	C. W. Clark	1 00
	W. H. Pennell	5 00
	H. B. Shattuck	5 00
	Mrs. Boynton, Medford	5 00
	P. B. Davis	5 00
	George Gage, Newburyport	1 00
	Livermore	1 00
	Cash	1 00
	Whichenton	50
	Clara Sharp	2 00
	Two Boys	1 00
Society in Kennebunk, Me., Rev. Mr. Lockwood		10 00
Brown.	Geo. P. Ammon, Hyde Park, for President	20 00
Congregational Church, Tewksbury		4 00
W. Hobbs.	Miss Wilson of Lynn	5 00
	Miss Severance of Lynn	5 00
	North Church	10 00
C. W.	W. J. Van Patten	10 00
D.D.	Choate Burnham	10 00
Rev. E. K. Alden,	Y. P. S. C. E., Williamstown, Mass.	5 00
Precious Pearl. Ceylon.	Rev. Dr. E. K. Alden	19 00
	Mrs. C. A. Perry	1 00
		———
Amount carried forward,		$2,003 00

Amount brought forward,	$2,003 00
C. G. Whaples, Humphrey street, New Haven	5 00
Rev. Alfred H. Hayes	20 00
Total	$2,028 00

The next exercise consisted of a practical illustration of the method of conducting a " Bible Training Class." David McConaughy, Jr., secretary of the Philadelphia Y. M. C. A., invited six young men to the platform and taking up certain portions of the scripture he examined his class in the various passages, bringing out by judicious questions the points which he wished to emphasize. Mr. McConaughy answered a number of questions put by members of the audience. The benediction by Rev. T. W. Jones, of Saratoga, closed the afternoon session.

WEDNESDAY EVENING.

After calling the conference to order, President Van Patten introduced Rev. Dr. Alden of Boston, Mass., who conducted the opening exercises of prayer and scripture reading.

After singing by the congregation and choir, President Van Patten introduced as the next speaker Rev. N. Boynton of Haverhill, who spoke on the first of the cardinal principles of our work, " Organization;" Rev. J. L. Hill of Lynn treated the next division of the topic, " Expression;" Rev. C. A. Dickinson of Lowell spoke on the third principle, " Diversion;" and Rev. F. E. Clark of South Boston discussed the last division, " Obligation." These addresses, which may be found in the Appendix, plainly and forcibly set forth the distinguishing features of the Christian Endeavor Society.

After a solo by Miss Vorn Holz, the congregation joined in singing the doxology, and were dismissed with the benediction by Rev. F. E. Clark.

THURSDAY FORENOON.

Rev. P. B. Davis of Hyde Park conducted the morning prayer-meeting. After a few words of encouragement and good advice to the young people, the meeting was thrown open, and a half hour was passed in earnest prayer and testimony. At 9.30 the Business Committee reported the order of exercises for the day, through its chairman, Secretary Ward. The report was accepted and adopted.

President Van Patten next called for the reports of the various committees. Mr. Brokaw, chairman of the committee on the secretary's report, said that the report was accurate and it was evident that Mr. Ward was the right man in the right place. The following resolution was presented and adopted :

Resolved, That in view of the necessity of having full and correct statistical tables in the hands of our general secretary, for publication, for the sake of knowing to whom to send literature, and also upon whom to draw for funds, it is hereby

Resolved, That the fifth annual conference not only calls especial attention to this matter, but also that it makes Mr. Ward's request its own request, hoping that such action and endorsement will suffice to insure careful compliance therewith from every society in existence.

Rev. Mr. Clark presented the report of the committee upon the president's address as follows :

We wish to express our sincere gratification with the tenor and spirit of the address and the many signs of progress which it reports. Aggressive, yet temperate and wise, we feel that it was the embodiment of mature thought and the expression of an earnest mind enlightened by experience. While there are many points which we should like to emphasize did time permit, there are three worthy of special attention, viz.: Our President's suggestion (1) concerning a Society Paper, (2) concerning the more complete organization of the work in state and county conventions, and (3) concerning the missionary work, which is rapidly assuming an important and most interesting phase.

On motion of Rev. J. L. Hill the report was accepted and placed on file.

OFFICERS ELECTED.

Rev. Mr. Adriance of the nominating committee presented the following :

President, W. J. Van Patten of Burlington, Vt. ; vice presidents, Rev. H. A. Stinson, D. D., St. Louis, Mo. ; Rev. C. F. Deems, D. D., New York city ; Rev. J. W. Dinsmore, D. D., of Bloomington, Ill. ; Rev. Alexander MacKenzie, D.D., of Cambridge, Mass. ; Rev. Erastus Blakeslee of New Haven, Conn. ; general secretary, Geo. M. Ward of Boston, Mass. ; treasurer, Wm. Shaw of So. Boston, Mass. ; clerk, W. H. Pennell of Portland, Me. ; auditor, A. W. Burnham of Lowell, Mass. ; Superintendents—Maine, Rev. A. T. Dunn, Portland ; New Hampshire, Rev. J. C. Rollins, Milford ; Vermont, George Perkins, W. B. Hazen, Hartford ; Massachusetts, A. H. Plumb, Boston, C. B. Newton, Hadley ; Rhode Island, C. F. Stevens, Providence ; Connecticut, Eli Manchester, Jr., New Haven ; New York, A. L. Graham, New York city, Rev. H. W. Sherwood, Syracuse, W. G. Bassett, Rochester ; New Jersey, Rev. J. C. Kerr, Elizabeth ; Pennsylvania, H. M. Kaisinger, Hatboro ; Ohio, A. D. Visscher, Springfield, C. J. Chase, Medina ; Illinois, C. B. Holdrege, Bloomington ; Iowa, Rev. C. A. Towle, Monticello ; Missouri, George B. Graff, P. M. Morgan, St. Louis ; Nebraska, Rev. G. W. Noble, Weeping Water ; Michigan, Rev. B. F. Sargent, Grand Rapids ; Wisconsin, F. J. Harwood, Appleton ; Kansas, E. D. Walker, Peabody ; Minnesota, Rev. E. M. Noyes, Duluth ; Arizona, Rev. C. S. Beardsley, Prescott ; Colorado, Rev. George Michael, Greeley ; California, Rev. J. Q. Adams, San Francisco, Pastor Westminster Church ; Texas, Duncan Hensley, Esq., 233 E. Houston street, San Antonio.

The report was accepted and the officers elected.

The General Secretary was instructed to fill the vacancies in the case of states not already provided for by the committee Rev. Mr. Dickinson for the committee on resolutions, reported as follows :

Your committee would report that their work during this session has not been specially burdensome, but a single case for consideration having been presented to them. It is quite natural that all friends of temperance should feel a deep interest in our work and should desire to identify themselves with it. It is generally understood that the Society of Christian Endeavor is in its spirit and aim a temperance organization. To emphasize this point it was recommended at the last convention, that a temperance committee be chosen in each local society. To meet the desires of our temperance friends who have urged this matter during the present session, your committee would call the attention of the convention to the temperance feature of our work, and recommend that, during the coming year, this work be pressed in our societies with vigor, and with special reference to extending its practical and scientific knowledge of the evils of intemperance, and impress upon our young people total abstinence principles.

On motion of Mr. Hill the report was accepted and adopted. At this point a communication was read from the Free St. Society of Portland, Me., pledging $10. It was received with applause.

Following the reports of committees Rev. S. W. Adriance presented an able paper on the musical contribution of the society to the church work. Coming as this did from one who is thoroughly posted in all that pertains to music, the suggestions offered were doubly valuable. The paper is printed in the Appendix.

Mr. Wm. Shaw of So. Boston, next presented a paper on The Promotion of Devotional Spirit; expedients, division bands, etc. This paper also is contained in the Appendix. After prayer by Rev. Mr. Robertson of Vergemes, Vt., on motion of Rev. Mr. Hill the papers just mentioned were referred to the executive committee. The next topic, on the duties of officers, was opened by Rev. W. E. Strong of Beverly, Mass. Mr. Strong ably set forth the need of tried and trained persons in all the offices connected with the society, and after dwelling on the necessity of such requirements, he showed the great advantage it would be to a church to have in their midst, members who had been trained by the duties required of them as officers in the society of Christian Endeavor.

J. T. Alling, Rochester, N. Y., followed the last speaker with a short paper on the duties of committees. Mr. Alling offered many valuable suggestions for the assistance of the various committees, and urged all to give their best efforts to the work of the committees to which they belonged.

A short discussion followed, which brought out many useful hints to be gained from the practical work of many of the societies represented.

Next followed, in order, papers on " Relation of Local Societies to the United Society," by George M. Ward, General Secretary; " Methods of Local Societies for Raising Money," written by George B. Graff, St. Louis, read by P. M. Morgan of St. Louis; " Associate Membership," by Rev. H. C. Hitchcock, Somerville, Mass. All of the above papers are printed in full in the Appendix. On motion of Rev. Mr Clark, Secretary Ward's paper was referred to a special committee consisting of Rev. F. E. Clark, Rev. P. B. Davis, Mr. C. B. Newton.

Rev. H. B. Grose here made an appeal to those present to become members of the U. S. C. E. Blanks were distributed among the audience, and a large number of names was secured. At this point Rev. Dr. Alden of Boston subscribed twenty dollars to make " Precious Pearl," a member of the society in Ceylon, a life member of the U. S. C. E. The generous offer was received with applause, and Dr. Alden himself was made a life member.

The session closed with benediction by Rev. Mr. Hitchcock.

THURSDAY AFTERNOON.

The session was opened by Rev. Mr. Bray of New Haven, Conn., who announced the hymn, after which a selection of Scripture was read and prayer offered.

The report of the committee on Mr. Ward's paper was made by Rev. F. E. Clark, Chairman. The report was adopted, as follows:

Realizing the importance of a vital connection being established between the local societies and the united societies, we recommend that the suggestions of our general secretariy be carrted out, and that in order to distribute the financial burden as evenly as possible over our large membership, the sum of ten cents per member from each society be expected from all those who receive the benefits of the united society, and that our secretary be instructed to communicate the desire of the convention on this subject to all the local societies who have not been represented in our conference.

Mr. Pennell, Clerk of the United Society, stated that it had been unanimously agreed upon to return to Saratoga Springs next year. The meetings will be held July 5, 6 and 7, 1887. The announcement was received with great applause.

Mr. Eli Manchester, Jr., of New Haven, Conn., presented a paper on "Local Union of Societies." The paper is contained in the Appendix.

The work of the Temperance Committee was the next topic for discussion. Miss Elizabeth T. Tobey, President of the Woman's Christian Temperance Union, opened the subject with a stirring appeal on behalf of the cause of temperance. She was followed by Miss Ida Clothier of Boston, who gave some startling but instructive facts with reference to the call which there was for work along this line. On motion of George W Frye of Lowell, the sentiments expressed by the two ladies were endorsed by a rising vote.

The next speaker was Rev. R. W. Brokaw of Belleville, N. J., whose paper on "Desirability of Conferences, State and Local," is printed in full in the Appendix.

Mr. Pennell moved that State conferences shall consider the matter of raising a general fund by the ten-cent contribution, and that the matter be the subject for discussion at State conferences. Carried.

Mr. Grose announced that the delegates of New York State had held a meeting, and appointed an executive committee, and called a State Conference to be held at Syracuse in December next.

On motion of Mr. Hill, the paper by Mr. Brokaw was referred to the Executive Committee with power.

Mr. Hoffman of Shelburne Falls, Mr. North of New Haven, Mr. Sykes of Lowell, Mr. Allen of Litchfield, Conn., Mr. Adriance of Lowell, Mr. Roblee of Michigan and Mr. Childs of North Manchester and others engaged in the discussion which followed.

Rev. C. F. Thwing of Cambridge, Mass., spoke on the subject, "How to Promote *Esprit de Corps*." It is a sentiment of war. It inspires to thought and action. The esprit de corps of this body is endeavor, work, toil, labor, &c. Not in the sense of the intellect, of soul, heart, but in the elevation and edification of the whole man in all the ages. This is the age of Christian Endeavor and this is the

motive of our labor here and in our homes. The way to promote it
is by work. We must work with the least evil result and most general good. We must work individual with individual. The best
work of the world is not done in the church, but by ourselves alone.
He entreated each one to extend a helping hand and lift up those
who are falling by the way.

The address was received with applause.

Rev. Mr. Boynton of Rye, N. H., made an earnest appeal for a
system of Bible study, and after explaining his views, requested that
his suggestions be referred to a special committee with power.

The motion was carried—" What are the special and most interesting
features of your work " and was made the topic for an open meeting.
The subject was opened by Rev. H. B. Grose of Poughkeepsie, N.
Y., who spoke of the work as conducted in his own church. The
first speaker was followed by Messrs. Nickerson of Glenville, Holdrege of Bloomington, Ill., Scott of Clinton, Shaw of South Boston,
Manchester of New Haven, Rice of Lee, and E. A. Hill of Syracuse.

The Question Box was opened by Rev. F. E. Clark. The box
contained many interesting questions all of which were answered
plainly and ably by " Father Endeavor " Clark. Miss Hills of So.
Boston, who was called upon to answer the question, " How shall we
induce our young ladies to take part in the meetings," replied at
once, " In just the same way as you would the young men." In
answer to some questions with reference to the training of the children in the work, Mrs. Slocum of Gilman, Iowa, gave an illustration
of her methods of conducting a meeting of her " Junior Society."

The session closed with the benediction by Rev. C. P. Mills of
Newburyport, Mass.

THURSDAY EVENING.

President Van Patten called the meeting to order and introduced
Rev. Mr. Livermore of Spencer, N. Y., who read the scripture lesson and was followed by Rev. Mr. Armes of Sunderland, who led
in prayer.

A report followed from the committee on credentials who had recorded representatives from 15 states, 129 towns, 148 societies.

The report was accepted, with the condition that the necessary
additions may be made to it.

The committee on resolutions submitted the following :

Resolved, That in urging societies to hold local and state conferences, it is not the
intention of this conference that these meetings be a burden on the hospitality of local
societies; but that it is our opinion that the principle of self-entertainment adopted
by the annual conference can also be adopted by local and state conferences to good
advantage.

Realizing the obligation under which the members of the fifth annual conference of
the United Society of Christian Endeavor have been placed by the many kind offices
of the Rev. T. W Jones, who for the past two months has been indefatigable in his
efforts to assist our secretary in preparing for this meeting,

Resolved, That we tender to him our most hearty thanks and assure him that we
deem it a privilege to welcome him to our society as one of its life members.

Adopted by a rising vote.

The speakers for the evening were then introduced. In place of Rev. T. L. Cuyler of New York, Rev. J. E. Rankin, D. D., of Orange, N. J., author of " Our National Hymn," made the opening address. He made a stirring appeal to all young Christians to become pupils of Christ and apprentices in the work of the Master. Rev. Dr. Twitchell of New Haven, was the next speaker. He congratulated the society on its growth and urged them to renewed efforts, predicting for them a most prosperous future. Rev. Dr. Alden of Boston, Mass., was the last speaker. After claiming to be an original member of the Christian Endeavor Society, the speaker went on to underlie the foundation of that organization and closed by urging those present to live up to their standard.

After a solo by Miss Burwell of New Haven, Conn., President Van Patten returned thanks to all present. In closing the fifth annual conference, he urged all to keep in close communion with the Master. Let us abide in His love by keeping His commandments.

" Keep Your Colors Flying " was then sung by the congregation, after which Dr. Twitchell pronounced the benediction. Following the conference a Christian Endeavor testimony meeting of about a half hour in length was held in the lecture room of the church.

PRESIDENT'S ADDRESS.

W. J. VAN PATTEN.

A year ago our faces were turned toward the sea, as we journeyed to the birthplace of the first society of our name — the beautiful city of Portland — near which, on the shores of the great Atlantic, we were to hold the fourth annual conference. The memory of that delightful time has surely been an inspiration and strength to all who participated, and has been a great incentive to bring us once more together to greet old friends and to make new ones. This year we have left the state and section of our birth as organizations, and have taken the first step toward the great centre of this nation, from whence, more than from any other part of the world, must issue the influences which shall shape and control the civilizing and Christian-izing forces that shall be, if God wills, the means of redeeming not only this land, but all this round earth, from the reign and power of sin. We are met in the place, yes, in the very building, already famous for assemblages drawn from all parts of the nation to confer about great enterprises; assemblages having high aims, looking to the upbuilding of the Kingdom of God, to planting the cross in waste places, and to the overthrow of evil by preaching the Gospel of the Saviour of mankind. We may congratulate ourselves upon being able to meet in this beautiful spot, and we should strive to gain much inspiration from what has already been accomplished by those that have met here before us. Let us be so greatly interested in all the meetings and work of this conference that the attractions and gaiety with which we are surrounded shall not draw us away from attend-ance upon every session.

A year has passed since we met, and to me is given the task of setting before you, so far as I may be able, the record made during that time by the Young People's Societies of Christian Endeavor. Have the bright anticipations formed during the enthusiastic meet-ings at Ocean Park been realized? Can those upon whom was placed the responsibility of office give a good account of their stew-ardship? Listen, I pray you, carefully to the various reports which will be presented, and judge how the work has been done! The first year of the United Society has also passed, and from its executive officer, the General Secretary, Mr. Ward, you have had more in detail a record of its work. The opening of the year found the Board of Trustees uncertain as to the future. The most important step taken at the Ocean Park conference was the move to employ a General Secretary. At the first meeting of the Board, they appointed a committee to seek out and recommend a suitable person for that office. At the next meeting, held a month later, they recommended

Rev. S. W. Adriance, and he was elected. He accepted the call to the office, but could not enter upon the work until November, which caused delay in much that should have had prompt attention. The printing of reports had also been delayed by what seemed unavoidable difficulties. At length Mr. Adriance entered upon his duties, but so great pressure was brought to bear upon him by his church that he almost immediately tendered his resignation. The Trustees were loath to accept it, for they had expected much from his administration of that office, and had waited long for him to take up the work. The office was tendered to Rev. Mr. Brokaw of New Jersey, but he could not bring himself to give up the work of the pastorate, although so greatly interested in the Young People's Societies of Christian Endeavor. Attention was then turned to the Treasurer, Mr. Ward, who had commended himself by his administration of his office, and by the interest and ability shown as one of the Board of Trustees. He was elected to fill the vacancy, and since December has performed the duties in a manner most satisfactory to the Board. The work of the office has been very large, correspondence pouring in from all parts of the country, asking innumerable questions in regard to the organization and methods of Christian Endeavor Societies. In addition to this was the labor of preparing and distributing printed matter, sending reports, &c., &c., all of which you can see has made your General Secretary a very busy man. If some have been disappointed in not hearing as much of his work as they expected, let them remember the great but unavoidable delay in filling the office, and the amount of accumulated work upon his hands, and the pressure ever since. Mr. Ward continued to act as Treasurer until May, when he resigned that office, and his place was filled by the election of Mr. William Shaw. The Board of Trustees have held six meetings — two in Portland and four in Boston — at each of which numerous matters have come up for discussion and decision. At the meeting in October Mr. J. W. Stevenson tendered his resignation as Secretary of the Board, and Mr. W. H. Pennell was elected to fill the vacancy, the Board being very glad to thus be able to avail themselves of the knowledge and zeal of our former honored President.

Let us turn now to consider what has been done by the United Society in promoting the growth and efficiency of the great number of Young People's Societies of Christian Endeavor scattered through our broad land. As you have learned from the report of the General Secretary, the first and most notable feature is the great growth in number of local societies — a growth exceeding our most hopeful anticipations. Last year our Secretary reported the number of societies upon his records as two hundred and fifty-three, scattered throughout twenty-four states, territories and provinces. Now he will report eight hundred and fifty societies in thirty-five states, territories and provinces, and seven in foreign lands. This gives over three-fold increase — a remarkable result in a movement of this kind, and one most gratifying to all having an interest in this method of promoting the growth of the church. This increase has been very general, so that now every section of the country is represented in our ranks; but it is a fact of no small significance that the largest growth has been, almost without exception, in the states where the work was best known, as an increase of two hundred and thirty societies in New England shows. If the work done in the last four years by the societies in this section has so commended itself to those churches watching it that they have become convinced of its usefulness and its power for good, and have gladly adopted it, does it not prove that the season of probation is past, and that now this society may properly take its place as one of the great permanent Christian organizations? The forces that have contributed to the great growth of the past year are many and varied. Not least among them was the spirit of enthusiasm and of loyalty to our work which was carried home by the delegates from our last conference. It was a grand thing to gather together such a number of earnest young Christians who were eager to do their Master service, and to give definite direction to their purpose along the line of work for their fellows. By their assistance in many directions, they have shown the great value of personal service in extending such a work as this, and to this we are indebted more than to anything else for the rapid spread of our societies. Almost every one of the older societies has been like a hive of busy workers, sending out those of its own number to form new societies, often in far distant places. A devoted young Christian who has felt the help and strength given to his spiritual life by the association of others with him working for the same ends, will be sure to make some move, when he takes up his abode in a new place, to start such a society as the one that has proved so beneficial in his past experience. He will be as a branch of the one vine, grafted upon a new stock, and ready to bear fruit in the new home. A true missionary zeal has been in many of the members that have gone out from our societies, and the work that they have done is worthy of recognition at our hands. It would be well if all those who are thus instrumental in starting new societies would report the facts to their old society, and from that it be reported to the United Society, and there recorded in due form. If all that has already been done in this way could be known, the record would be a noble one.

Another means that has contributed greatly to the growth of societies has been the holding of conferences, union meetings and anniversaries. By these means the attention of other churches has been gained, and having seen the interest manifested and heard of the good work done, the formation of new societies has followed as a natural result. I wish to urge most strongly the holding of State Conferences, early in the autumn wherever it can be done. There are now twelve states where there are more than twenty societies. In each of these states it will be feasible to hold a State Conference, and the good that may result from it is plainly illustrated by what has been accomplished in the State of Connecticut the past year. At our conference one year ago, there were reported seventeen societies organized in that state. A few earnest delegates were in attendance from these societies, and they went home determined to do their best to greatly increase this number. A State Conference was called to meet November 18, widespread notice was sent through the columns of the press, and by circulars and correspondence. A large gathering, full of life and enthusiasm, was the result. From that time the formation of new societies went on rapidly, and now the number upon our roll for this state is seventy-five, or nearly five times that of one year ago. The holding of local conferences, of union meetings and anniversaries has also been a prominent feature of the work in both Connecticut and Massachusetts, and has done much to promote it, and to place these states in the van of the Christian Endeavor movement. If our societies existed all through the country in the same proportion, instead of eight hundred societies we should have eight thousand. If in this great State of New York we had the same proportion, we should have here seven hundred societies, instead of eighty-five. Let us, then, by all the means in our power, promote these gatherings, and let their stimulating effect be felt in the churches that have not yet tried the Christian Endeavor work, and beneficial results would follow as surely as they have in the states named.

The publication of a large number of the reports of the last conference, and their wide circulation, has done much to spread the knowledge of our work, and promote the formation of new societies. Ten thousand copies of the minutes, with the official reports, and two thousand full reports of the last conference, have been distributed to churches of all the leading evangelical denominations. In addition to this, a large number of articles have appeared in the religious papers, as well as many reports of meetings and conferences in secular papers. This all has greatly aided the growth of the movement. Especial acknowledgment should be made of the liberality of the Golden Rule of Boston. Its editor has carried out in letter and in spirit the offer made at the last conference, and has given the department devoted to the Christian Endeavor Societies ample space and prominent position. The knowledge thus gained by various societies of the methods used by others, and the interchange of ideas and items of interest, has been of much value.

But in speaking of the many causes of the great growth during the past year, we must not leave out of the account the labor of our General Secretary, who, by his correspondence and by his personal attendance at conferences and anniversaries, has done much to stimulate it; nor must we forget the unwearied interest and work of Mr. Clark, Mr. Dickinson, Mr. Hill, Mr. Brokaw, Mr. Pennell, and a large number more of pastors and laymen who have always been ready to render timely assistance. And finally, above all, and through all, and more than all, has been the working of God's Spirit, to whom be all honor and glory for the blessings granted. The most flourishing societies have been started, the most urgent calls for help and information have come from places where revivals have brought many to a new knowledge of the love of God in Christ Jesus, our Lord. These revived Christians and new converts, alike, have gladly taken upon themselves our pledges, and have lived up to the letter and spirit of their obligations. Oh! for a great tide of revival spirit all over our broad land, awakening every church to its duties and its opportunities, and leaving in its wake these societies to insure the Christian nurture of the little ones, and to train up a generation that will not be one of silent Christians, but of those that will be able and willing both to speak and work for their Master.

We have seen what has been the growth of the Christian Endeavor movement, as indicated by the increase in the number of the societies, and have reviewed the influences which have brought about this increase. What else has been accomplished by the Christian zeal and spirit of all these thousands of devoted young disciples of Christ? I wish that I knew the history of the last year of their loyal service! I would that I could set before you, in glowing periods, how, by fervent prayer, by tender word, by loving act, these young hearts have gone out to serve in the harvest field, heeding their Master's call; how they have come back with rejoicing, bringing their sheaves with them; but these things we can know but in part, though enough is known probably to each of us to fill our hearts with thankfulness, and to create a great hope within us for the future. There are, however, certain things of which we can take note. Pastors and churches have borne willing testimony to the help this plan of work for young Christians has been to them. As one said in a recent communication to a religious journal: "Multitudes of pastors find this society of inestimable importance in training Christian workers and prayer-meeting supporters. It should have the sympathy and support of our churches and of our religious papers, because of its loyalty to Jesus Christ and to His church, and because of the quality and abundance of its fruit." Many times has the personal testimony come to your officers that the Young People's Society of Christian Endeavor has been the life of some church, and the most encouraging feature in the religious outlook of the community. They have been referred to in religious conventions of different denominations, as "special causes of religious interest," as "a constant power for good," and as "schools for Christian nurture." These words would not be spoken if the societies represented had not been doing praise-worthy service in and for the churches with which they are connected, and we have the right to believe that what is true of these is true of a large majority of all that are formed throughout the land.

The growth of Christian unity, by the close fellowship that membership in sister societies has given young Christians, is one of the distinct gains made in the past year. This is especially noticeable where regular union meetings of the societies have been held, or where union organizations exist. The great value and promise of this union in and for Christian service should lead to the formation of many local unions and the promotion of united effort by the churches. In a few places in our land, the power of united, organized work by the Christian churches has been tried, and its ability to solve many of the most perplexing problems of the day has been tested. Will not the union of the Endeavor Societies of a place or section lead to and aid in this united Christian effort which we so greatly need? We do not realize what power our churches would have if banded together in a compact whole for aggressive effort, instead of being so many separate companies, often indifferent to each other's success. It is my most earnest hope and expectation that these Young People's Societies, by their natural affiliation, without regard to their church relation, will do much to bring about this union of the whole body of Christ's followers.

We have been pleased to note, during the past year, that the fear in regard to the tendency of this movement, which some pastors and churches have manifested, has nearly passed away. Many who have tried it doubtingly have become its earnest advocates, and when any rise to criticise, are its quick defenders. We no longer hear that the society seeks to displace the church, or that its members forget what they owe the church, but such words as these, which recently appeared in a leading paper, show the present drift of opinion. Speaking of a local society, it was said: "Our society is no more a distinct organization from the church than the infant department is distinct from the Sunday school. Our society is in the closest relation to the church; is simply the church at work in this particular direction, and is to-day the very hope of the church."

And now, turning from the past with full hearts, as we remember all that it has brought to us of privilege and blessing, and taking from it the lessons gained by experience, let us survey the future, striving to see what it demands at our hands, and what it may have in store for us.

The experience of the year just ended shows that the plans adopted at Ocean Park were wise. The work that has flowed in upon the General Secretary has fully tasked his time and strength. It could not have been done by any voluntary labor which we could command, nor could we ask anyone to assume such a burden except as a paid officer. So the wisdom and necessity of that part of our plan has been proved. We are fortunate in having as General Secretary one who had real enthusiasm and great aptitude for his work, and I trust that he may still continue in this office. As our first duty, then, the future demands that we provide financial support to the Board of Trustees, so that the experiment of employing a General Secretary may be made the settled aim and purpose of the United Society.

The financial problem does not seem a large one. Four thousand dollars is estimated to be sufficient to meet all the necessary expenses of the central organization, and with a constituency of a thousand societies, as we shall have this year, this sum should be easily and quickly secured. But for many reasons, all these local societies are not to be depended upon. A great many have been formed without aid from the United Society, and do not feel the obligation of helping to support it. Many are without any financial plans, and have no funds which they can vote for the purpose, and in very many instances our appeal does not go to the person who should or could bring it before the society for action. So the usual result is that less than one-fourth of the societies respond to the call for assistance, and the most of these with but small amounts. Our plans for securing life and annual members of the United Society should bring in a considerable amount, but they fail from the same cause — our inability to get persons to push them with the local societies. It can be easily seen that the financial problem is one that needs earnest attention. Our work must grow more and more aggressive, and increased work always entails increased expense. Our work must not and shall not lag for want of funds, and if each society here represented will give hearty support as they may be able, all that may be needed can be raised.

Another demand which the future makes of us is for better and more abundant literature, and for a periodical devoted to our interests. It seems to me that it cannot be doubted that such a paper as would meet the wants of the membership would receive adequate support, and would prove a most valuable adjunct to our work ; therefore I would recommend that the subject be referred to the proper committee for earnest consideration.

Another demand that the work has upon its leaders is a continuance of their watchful care and kindly guidance. It would be strange if in so widespread a movement, taken up in many places without adequate knowledge, and often, when organized, wholly left in the hands of the young and inexperienced, there should not be some failures. The wonder is that there have been so few. There is no good reason why there should be failure anywhere, unless so few young people remain in a church that a meeting for a half hour cannot be maintained, even when all take part. As one vigorous friend of the work has said : " Whenever a society fails, there is always a reason for it ; sometimes popery in the pulpit ; sometimes pugnacity in the deacons ; sometimes perverseness among the young people."

And now what has the future in store? Look out over our broad land, with its tens of thousands of Christian churches, with the millions of little ones gathered in its Sunday schools. Think of the good work that has been done in the few societies that have been organized long enough to have tested their work, to see " whether it be of man, or whether it be of God ;" and then think of what would be the effect if even the half of these churches were using the Christian force which exists, though almost unknown, in the millions of the young they are training in their schools ! Would not the cause of our Lord, who showed such love for the little ones, be advanced marvellously ? Instead of scattered showers of blessing through special efforts, would not there be a continuous and widespread coming of the young to the blessed Saviour ? How our hearts expand as we think of the wonderful possibilities ! Let us nerve ourselves for the work, and resolve, by the grace and strength granted from on high, to push forward, ready to do all that lays in our power to expand the activities and extend the influence of young Christians. And our thought and purpose should not be confined to working with the churches, or in our own land.

The great "Problem of the Country Town" is still unsolved. It is scarcely more than stated, and he will be a wise, yes, an inspired man, who shall be able to successfully answer it. But may not the organization of Young People's Societies of Christian Endeavor be one step towards the solution in some places?

Less than three weeks ago I went, with a few others, to a school-house a few miles from town, where a mission Sunday school had been carried on for some time. The teaching of the Word and the prayer of faith had prevailed, and several of the scholars had been hopefully converted. Too remote from church to enjoy many of its privileges, it was a serious question as to what should be done to promote their Christian growth and insure their faithfulness. A Society of Christian Endeavor was proposed. Its methods were explained and recommended. The young people signified their willingness to accept the rules, and when we met to organize, they were enthusiastic over the new society, A good work is sure to be done there, and a neighborhood which a short time ago was apparently without spiritual life or inclination, stupid, dull and most unpromising, will be made bright, active and full of spiritual promise for the future. Now, why cannot this be duplicated in thousands of places all over our land? Not to take the place of churches, but to prepare the way for them, or to give spiritual life in localities where churches could not be supported. I believe this to be a line of development worthy our thoughtful attention and fostering care wherever it can be started.

Another sphere in which the usefulness of the societies has already been tested is in connection with educational institutions.

The work done by the Young Men's Christian Associations in colleges and universities is of vast importance. I believe it to be one of the most hopeful features of the present religious movement of the country. To-day two hundred representatives of college associations are gathered in Northfield, Mr. Moody's Massachusetts home, to spend a large part of their vacation with that wonderful man in the study of the Bible, and to learn of its power and beauty from those who are examples of what God's Word can make those who believe it and study it. All these go back to their colleges for two years or more of school life. What a power for good! What an inspiration they may be to their fellow-students! Skilled workmen will they be in the Master's vineyard, and much fruit will they gather in.

But the work of the Young Men's Christian Associations in the higher institutions can be grandly supplemented in thousands of schools and academies by the Young People's Societies of Christian Endeavor In it both sexes can join, and all ages, and the training the young will there receive will prepare them for greater usefulness in the Associations in the college, or the church at home.

The knowledge that a good society of this kind exists in the school to which they are going would be a pleasant thing to the young members of our local societies as they are leaving home; and to the parents it will give a feeling of security and hope for the future that nothing else could equal. Let this, then, be one of the directions in which our work in the time to come shall extend. We have in the last few days received a letter full of hope for the future of the work of our societies in missionary fields. Miss M. W. Leitch has already formed three societies, having nearly two hundred members, in the Island of Ceylon, and hopes to form a number more before the end of the year; also to go to Southern India, and start the movement there. She says: "If this movement could be really started in mission fields, this clear idea of working for the conversion and ingathering of the young, I believe it would promote the growth of the work as nothing else would, for the hope of the church, in mission lands, even more than at home, is the young."

And now for what do you think she asks? It is not for money, it is not for books, but it is for a *man.* Listen: "Can you not send an evangelist around the world to form Young People's Societies of Christian Endeavor in every mission field, and introduce the idea to every missionary?

"Here is a grand object to set before your Union of the Societies of Christian Endeavor, something in their own line for which they can give and for which they can pray. Who could measure the untold good which might, which would, result if the work in mission lands was directed more toward the children? This great work your Society *can* do. Will it?"

Is that not a wide open door, and a warm invitation? Yes! an earnest urging to enter in?

Look through that door and beyond, and what may we see? In the not far distant future, Societies of Christian Endeavor encircling the world, binding together Christian hearts, and hastening the time when a united church shall have overthrown the idols of the heathen, and the Lord Christ shall reign everywhere.

Societies have also been founded by mission churches in China and most cheering words come to us from them. Everywhere where our missionaries are gathering the little ones into Sabbath schools and teaching to pray and praise, the Young People's Societies of Christian Endeavor can be made an effectual means of Christian nurture. So, too, in all Protestant lands of whatever tongue we should scatter the good seed, and we may hope before many years to see it bearing much fruit to the honor and glory of our God. I trust a permanent mission committee may be formed who shall have charge of these matters, and upon whose recommendations we can wisely act in the future.

The work to be done by the officers and trustees the coming year will be much the same as in the year past. The papers and discussions to be brought before this conference may develope new directions or methods which it may be desirable to pursue.

Whatever you may deem wise to direct, you may be sure will be carried out with all the zeal and faithfulness of which they are capable.

Let us recognize the bright prospects before us, giving thanks to Him who has called us to such a glorious service, and taking courage from what we have so far been able to accomplish, push forward with fresh zeal, and with full faith in the promises of the blessed Lord who said, " Lo, I am with you alway, even to the end of the world."

SPECIAL REPORT FROM CONNECTICUT.

BY REV. ERASTUS BLAKESLEE, OF NEW HAVEN.

A year ago there were reported from the State of Connecticut but 17 societies, with less than 1,000 members ; now we can report about 80 societies, with more than 4,000 members.

This remarkable growth resulted in part from the natural tendency of the society to propagate itself, every society becoming in some sort the parent of others ; in part from the influence of the United Society and their efficient General Secretary ; and in part from our local efforts.

It is to some brief statements regarding these local efforts that I now ask your attention.

Your delegates from Connecticut went home from the conference at Old Orchard last year with a feeling of responsibility concerning the progress of the work in that State. On consultation, the most feasible thing appeared to be a State convention at New Haven in November, to be called by the pastors and presidents of the New Haven societies ; with intent, both to get together the various societies already organized, and also to spread such information about the Y. P. S. C. E., and to excite such interest in it, as should lead to the formation of new societies. The representatives of the New Haven societies fell in with this plan most cordially, the Humphrey street society offering its hospitalities for the occasion.

In the call to the convention, all the societies in the State, and all pastors and others interested, were invited. This invitation, with the program, was sent to upwards of 500 churches ; and in addition, special invitations were sent to more than 100 pastors. A short statement of the origin, growth, objects and methods of the Y. P. S. C. E. was put into print and sent to about 100 newspapers, with a request for notice. Most, if not all, kindly responded by printing

the article wholly or in substance. In these various ways it is believed that the coming convention and the society it represented
were brought to the attention of about everybody in the State likely
to be interested therein.

The convention was a great success. There were 208 pastors and
delegates present, representing all the societies already organized,
and many churches in which none had then been formed. Our well
known Y. P. S. C. E. friends, the Rev. Messrs. Dickinson, Adriance and Brokaw, were present and assisted us greatly. The program was arranged with a view to give information about the Y. P.
S. C. E., and to excite interest in it, rather than to discuss methods.
It was taken for granted that the society as now organized is on a
sound basis, and no questions were raised as to special matters.

At this meeting a very simple preliminary State organization was
effected by the appointment of an Executive Committee of seven,
who, with the President, Secretary and Treasurer, were entrusted
with all business for the ensuing year. It is expected that at the next
State convention in October, some more permanent organization
will be made.

The effect of this convention, full reports of which were published
in the daily and weekly papers, was most marked. New societies
began to spring up at once in every direction ; not less than fifty in
all during the forty weeks from then till now, and more to follow.

The other most valuable special feature of our work in Connecticut has been the formation of CHRISTIAN ENDEAVOR UNIONS, of
which full reports will be made here to-morrow. Only let me say in
passing, that our New Haven union is the most efficient aid we have
in promoting the interests of our societies in that vicinity. It now
includes twelve societies, every one of which, I think, would testify
to its inspiring influence. In that respect its meetings are in kind,
locally, what this conference is, nationally.

A similar union of four societies, has just been formed in Manchester, which starts off most vigorously, and promises to become an
important factor in Y. P. S. C. E. work in that region. We heartily
commend the organization of similar unions among local societies everywhere, as likely to mark an important forward step in the
development of the Christian Endeavor idea.

Pardon me if I have seemed over particular in stating the special
features of our work in Connecticut. It has been in the hope of
stimulating others to do likewise. If our growth there has been
specially significant, it has not been for causes which may not easily
be set in operation elsewhere.

THE USE OF HYMN SINGING IN THE MEETINGS OF THE YOUNG PEOPLE'S SOCIETY OF CHRISTIAN ENDEAVOR.

BY REV. CHARLES PERRY MILLS, NEWBURYPORT, MASS.

A Secretary of a Young Men's Christian Association was once invited by your essayist to address his Sunday evening congregation. Immediately at the close of the address your essayist, all inadvertently, arose and said : " We will now sing ' Hallelujah, 'tis done ! ' " If that phrase should leap spontaneously to your lips at the close of this paper, your emotion would be pardonable, for this subject of hymn singing in our meetings has been committed to unskillful hands and yet, venturing as best he may, the following treatment of the theme is offered :

1. · To speak of the use of hymn singing that is common to all prayer-meetings. By no one has the true nature and functions of hymns been better suggested or defined than by St. Paul. In writing to the Ephesians he says : " Be filled with the Spirit ; speaking to yourselves in psalms and hymns and spiritual songs, singing and making melody in your heart to the Lord." In a similar strain he writes to the Colossians ; " Let the word of Christ dwell in you richly in all wisdom ; teaching and admonishing one another in psalms and hymns and spiritual songs, singing with grace in your hearts to the Lord." From these rich words it appears that hymns have two sides, their side for God and their side for man. It inheres then in the nature and belongs to the function of a hymn to express the emotions of a worshipping heart toward God. The devout soul adores God for His gentle and majestic greatness ; it thanks Him for His providential and gracious goodness ; it supplicates the tokens of His favor ; it aspires after His likeness. By an irrepressible impulse the melody of the heart breaks out into the melody of song. Herein is indicated the origin of hymns and, at the same time, their primary use, viz., as ascriptions of glory, as acclamations of thanksgiving, as prayers of petition and communion.

The secondary use of hymns is for the edification of man. Under this aspect, their first use is as a means of instruction. Christian doctrines are adapted for singing as well as preaching. The holy men of God of olden time, who spake as they were moved by the Holy Ghost, in order to teach divine truth, were some of them prophets and some of them singers. Moreover, the great truths of the New Testament were put immediately, with simple and stirring grandeur, into the songs of the early church, and ever since have been taught and maintained quite as much by songs as by creeds. Truth sung is more powerful than truth spoken, and a hymn in the memory will go on teaching long years after a sermon has been forgotten. Said Andrew Fletcher: "I knew a very wise man that believed that if a man were permitted to make all the ballads, he need not care who should make the laws of a nation." So great is the teaching power of Christian song that we are not to judge as very wide of the mark the paraphrase of this famous saying, which has been made as applicable to a Christian poet: "If I can make all the hymns of Christians, I care not who writes their creeds or preaches their sermons."

Again, hymns in their secondary aspect, have use for exhortation, comfort, warning, inspiration. In short, we address and admonish one another in hymns. The address is not directly so much to the thoughts of the intellect as to the sensibilities of the heart. To Augustine's definition, "a hymn is praise to God in the form of song," we must add, it is also exhortation to man. Augustine himself is an illustration of the manward side of hymns, for of his first entrance into church at Milan, after conversion, he records this experience: "The voices flowed in at my ears, truth was distilled in my heart, and the affection of piety overflowed in sweet tears of joy." Hymns thus not only express, but they also excite, religious emotions. They quicken feeling to favor the surrender of the will *in* conversion, and they arouse it to sustain the soul *after* conversion. By them the mind is prepared for truth to be spoken, and beyond the utmost reach of the truth that has been spoken they lift the soul into holy ecstasies. The early Christians, the unsurpassed confessors and martyrs of the church, provoked themselves to ardor and steadfastness by their songs; the Reformers braved buffet and gave battle, inspired by the conquering power of the songs of Luther that rolled and surged in heroic measure; and the Methodists aroused the religious apathy of England and America by the inflammatory influence of Wesley's lyrics. Aids to the culture of personal piety, wings for the soul to lift itself above the religion of the intellect, flames burning their bright way to the remotest feelings of the heart, stimulants to holy ardor and endeavor, outlets of joy, inlets of spiritual impression, bugle notes sounding as for war—these phrases, in lieu of extended illustration, may picture the manifold uses of hymns common to all religious meetings.

> "God sent His singers upon earth
> With songs of sadness and of mirth,
> That they might touch the hearts of men
> And bring them back to heaven again."

2. To speak of the use of hymn-singing that is distinctive to the meetings of the Society of Christian Endeavor. Proportionately larger and freer use should be made of this means of worship than in the ordinary meetings of the church. That this should be so is suggested by the natural love of young people for singing. Unrepressed youth must sing, spontaneously, frequently, spiritedly. At a depressing period of the Civil War, when the National troops were losing ground and falling back, the Government at Washington proposed to economize by reducing the number of the bands of music;

but the generals in the field sent quick remonstrance and pleaded for. more music, promising, by its cheering and inspiring aid, more triumphs. The bands were multiplied, and victories soon advanced our standards. At a critical moment, when the soldiers of Napoleon were about to yield to the fatigues of their wearisome march over the Alps, he revived their energies by ordering the bands to strike up the national anthem. Cromwell also, suffusing patriotism with the sublime sentiment of religion, led his Ironsides into victorious battle to the music of " Praise God, from whom all blessings flow." We pity the mournful fanaticism that inspired the Children's Crusade, but whose heart does not thrill before the historic picture of five thousand children embarking from Marseilles, singing with insuppressible fervor, *Veni Creator Spiritus?* History has demonstrated the power of song to kindle the enthusiasm of large bodies of men, and especially to fire the energies of youth; if, therefore, we aim to make the Endeavor Society a movement of Christian victory, we must make it instinct with the spirit and life of singing. It is true that young people, in the conduct of meetings, will sometimes use hymns simply as episodes of worship, or to relieve themselves of the responsibilities of more difficult parts, such as praying and speaking, but wise leadership will readily correct any infelicity or disproportion that may occur. As a rule, even young people will need the spur more than the curb.

Again, hymn-singing has use in our meetings to foster the emotions which our society seeks to cultivate. Be it understood by all concerned, that the Endeavor Society is not a sentimental association; it has a policy. Neither is it a narrow conception, promoting a lean type of Christian character; like the city above, it lieth four-square, the length, the breadth and the height of it being equal. What, then, are the emotions which it aims to express and excite? The first emotion which we cultivate is the emotion of praise to Christ as our Redeemer and King, for ours is a Society of *Christian* Endeavor. Its head, heart, body, is Christ. It is not for us to praise God as do the angels that excel in strength, nor as did Adam in innocency; it is ours, rather, to praise Him in Christ as do the redeemed in heaven. The burden of the celestial song is to ascribe glory and dominion unto the Lamb that was slain, who, through the sceptre of the cross, has become the King of saints. In imitation of that song, we are to sing the glories of His love, the triumphs of His cross, the majesties of His reign.

> "I've found the pearl of greatest price,
> My heart doth sing for joy;
> And sing I must, for Christ is mine—
> Christ shall my song employ."

But Christ is not to us merely a subject of thought, nor yet alone an object of affection; He is the prime motive and the supreme end of our work. So that the Christian idea, which is the very essence and the only vitality of the Endeavor movement, works itself out in four cardinal principles. The first principle is organization. The young people band themselves together in mutual loyalty to Christ.

Very quickly does the sentiment of union tend to solidify by the use of those hymns which, through constant employment, become the character hymns of the Society. The Constitution and By-Laws ot the Society make it what Adam was before God breathed into him the breath of life, viz.: a lifeless organization; but when the Society is stirred by some inspiring hymn that awakens all voices and kindles all hearts with kindred feelings, it then becomes what Adam was after he received the breath of life, viz.: a living organism. A people realize the national feeling more vividly in a national air than in their national Constitution. Not long since your essayist heard the Hungarian Gypsy Band play the Hungarian War March, and while listening to its thrill and pathos, he could well believe the statement that no patriot of the land of Kossuth could hear that martial anthem without rising to his feet and wishing to fall in rank with all compatriots for battle. A spirit akin to this a good hymn starts in a meeting of the Society of Christian Endeavor where the young people have enlisted under the banner of Christ.

Another cardinal principle of our work is expression. Silence is not a virtue that we cultivate. It grows without cultivation. We aim at the expression of Christian feeling. Pre-eminent among the denominations for utterance is the Methodist, and it has been able to secure such freedom of the voice in prayer and testimony largely through its free use of the voice in Christian song. This one illustration, so striking, may suffice to show that while hymn-singing serves direct purposes in our meetings, it also indirectly stimulates to participation in the other exercises. The high places of heaven, or, according to the quaint line of an old-time hymnist, " Every bright rafter of the mighty hereafter," will be vocal with happy singers, full of adoring sentiments that find fit expression only in anthems of praise ; so, in anticipation of the celestial chorus, let the thanksgivings, ascriptions, aspirations that throb in the hearts of our young people come to expression not alone in remark or prayer, but also in joyous hymn.

Sociability is the third principle of our work. This feature is manifested in many ways, but how, it may be confidently asked, is the spirit of it better created and forwarded than by singing hymns of fellowship? The thought of the communion of believers and of fellow-helpers to the truth has entered into numerous hymns, and it is the use of such hymns that must be relied on to establish that social feeling and *esprit de corps,* without which any society is a rope of sand. Who that was ever a member of a college class fails to recall how heart was knit to heart and faith pledged to faith by the college songs that were sung in class-room or on campus? And how thrillingly is the memory of college days kept alive by the singing of these songs again in the intervals of life's busy work. Given the free use of appropriate hymns, and every local Endeavor Society will be not a whit behind a college class in the spirit of social union, which is a spirit of joy and power.

Obligation is the fourth principle upon which our work proceeds.

We bind ourselves by pledges. We voluntarily subscribe to a constitution that demands christian endeavor. We are not societies of heavenly rest; we aim to create a stir, to start and push a movement. Aggressive piety undergirded with restraints and safeguards, but shotted with life and energy, is the type we favor. The mild virtues we promote, but are careful that they abound in reserve power that, when touched by occasion, they may spring, minerva-like, fully equipped in armored form. Imitators of degenerate Sampson we will not be; as Isaac Watts poetizes the story:

> "So Sampson, when his hair was lost,
> Met the Philistines to his cost;
> Shook his vain limbs with sad surprise,
> Made feeble fight and lost his eyes."

Rather, we pray with the Psalmist: "O God, how long shall the adversary reproach? Why withdrawest thou thy hand, even thy right hand? Pluck it out of thy bosom." And we enter into the spirit of this prayer as expressed by Sternhold and Hopkins' version of 1562:

> "Why dost thou withdraw thy hand aback
> And hide it in thy lappe?
> O pluck it out and be not slack
> To give thy foes a rappe."

The question now arises, how this sense of obligation, this spirit of aggression is to be aroused. The live singing of live hymns will do it. As the battle hymn of the Republic inflames patriotism and creates, as if by magic, soldiers ready for fight, so the principle of obligation, the most strenuous feature of our work, will be kept vivid and vital by the use of some of the grand tones of the church, such as, "All hail the power of Jesues' name," or, "Stand up for Jesus, ye soldiers of the cross."

In conclusion, the query is raised whether the time is not about ripe for a selection of hymns especially adapted for the Society of Christian Endeavor. The church, the prayer-meeting, the Sunday school has each its own selections; these selections have much in common, but still to each department there belongs a characteristic function that has called forth separate hymns and tunes. Would not the interests of our Societies be helped in every way if, out of the riches of hymnology, an appropriate compilation should be made in our behalf? Is the suggestion untimely that a committee be appointed to report at the sixth annual conference on a Christian Endeavor song-book; in the meantime receiving suggestions and passing judgment on original hymns and tunes that may be sent in? The singing of an inappropriate hymn constitutes sometimes what Dr. Johnson would call a "risible absurdity." Take, for example, an incident in the history of the class of 1879 of Andover Theological seminary. We were assembled in ordinary class prayer-meeting. All present were bachelors, bachelors of arts, being graduates of colleges, but apart from that we were bachelors in the plain and forlorn sense; and yet, by some unaccountable mischance, we blundered into singing a baptismal hymn:

> " Heavenly Father ! May thy love
> Beam upon us from above;
> Let this infant find a place
> In thy covenant of grace." ’

That hymn was too old for us by a number of years. Now, our young people must have appropriate hymns, neither those adapted to children, nor those to old age, but those congenial to youth. One feature only is wanting to make the time fully ripe for a Christian Endeavor Song Book, viz., that this movement, strange to say, has not yet called forth special hymns, so far as is known by your essay-ist. We wait for their appearance, we invite them to come, and we now send out word to all Christian poets among us to cultivate muse that we may have at least a few hymns that will embody the spirit and life of our society. That this occasion might be signalized by the appearance of the first hymn that the Society of Christian Endeavor has inspired, the writer applied to Rev. J. E. Rankin, D. D., of Orange, New Jersey, to produce it. Entering into the spirit of the request he kindly complied, and it is now not only with great pleasure that it is made public, but with equal confidence that, when sung to the tune of St. Gertrude, in its pure form, it will prove valu-able as a banner hymn, and an admirable beginning of an original Christian Endeavor hymnology.

EXPRESSION.

BY REV. JAMES L. HILL.

There is a peculiar relevancy between my theme and the sugges-tions of that day on which many of us made our journey hitherward to this queen of summer resorts. " The day we celebrate " is not associated with the beginnings of the idea of American Independence. " There is not," said John Adams, " an idea in the Declaration made upon the Fourth of July, but was already backneyed in Congress. The revolution was effected before the war commenced." Nor are we found rejoicing over the beginnings of our self-government under the Constitution. We had no help from that instrument in rallying our forces and in defending our rights. It was expected that the Amer-ican Administration of affairs would begin under the principles of the Articles of Confederation. It was for a revision of these articles that the convention was called, which, finding that work impracticable, gave us the Constitution of the United States. Am I not right then in affirming, and there is religious power in what is thus proven, that the seven long weary sanguinary years of the Revolutionary War were fought through to a glorious triumph upon the basis of a *declaration*. The force that carried the colonies through was in the *embodied* idea. The *expression* of the idea gave it birth, fired it with a destiny and gave it unwonted energy. You will observe that it is from the standpoint of a Declaration that all our revolutionary history is reviewed. Here the unformed sentiment or the forming sentiment crystalized. Henceforth we deal in history with a new fact. Men must be given a place on which to stand when they would lift the world. So is it in religious life. Congregations break forth with singing when men *declare* their faith. I suppose that in the case of many persons there are a great many religious sentiments and convictions lying loose about the mind. A movement toward expression would bring them into line.

There are the children of Israel coming up out of bondage. They approach Jericho. Upon what is the preservation of Rahab and of her house made to depend? Not upon her faith, but rather upon the *expression* of her faith. The scarlet thread must be thrown out from the window *in token of her faith*. When we speak of yielding testimonies to our fellow men, we are prone to think first of the good that will be done to others. Let me turn that thought around. I want to make it evident that the primary advantage is to the one who thus adds by confession the seal to his faith. Indeed, I may say that it is not a living faith until it is expressed. Here is an egg; by sight or by sound you ascertain that there is life in the egg. It must be expressed, not only on account of those whom the fledgling may greet with its song, but there must be manifestation for the well-being of the life itself. Here is a tree. If insects strip the leaves away, which are its form of manifestation, it will some time, if expression is persistently denied, die in its place. Look at this seed; life is in it. The power of the germ, however, may be lost in time if you refuse it a chance of expression. Plant it. Let it manifest itself, and the earth will never be without that form of life. Neither can faith maintain its vitality except it is given an outward manifestation. Indeed, "faith without works *is dead*." Religious life without expression is incomplete. The expression is a part of the faith, it is the development or final stage of it. The Apostle does not say, "Thou shalt be saved if thou shalt believe in thine heart." That would recognize and reward a partial process. He insists rather upon a completed process as the terms on man's part, of salvation and so lays down these inseparable conditions of confession with the mouth as well as belief in the heart. Hence he continues that it is "with the mouth confession is made unto salvation." "Upon this Rock"—upon this solid foundation, not upon Peter's faith, for an undeveloped faith is a very insecure thing, but upon faith as it was that moment confessed—"I will found my Church." The faith of a man needs to be pronounced in order to hold the man. It is upon this idea that we proceed in laboring to secure temperance and other pledges. We want souls to commit themselves, and that for their own good. We instinctively distrust mere matters of sentiment and kindly disposition until they have become affirmative. This moral positiveness is of itself invaluable, and in the very work of manifestation we increase our facility and our value in those realms in which expression is so much desired.

And for this reason Christianity is not so much a **science as it is an art.** A science is only a systematic and orderly arrangement of knowledge where the best that can be said for a man is that he knows for the sake of knowing.

Our object is not to teach men what is good, but it is rather to *make* men good, to teach them TO BE good. It is to know for the sake of *doing*. An art is only acquired by the practice of it. It tends toward production and toward performance. A virtue can only be learned by practice. Godly characters are attained in the same way. One learns to read by reading, to write by writing, to pray by praying, and to do church work by serving upon committees and by engaging practically in useful labors. The tendency of an art is, as has often been shown, to work itself out into a system of rules which facilitate performance. The various committees into which our societies resolve themselves are but so many avenues for the practical manifestation of the religious energies and genius of young disciples. By these facilities, we come into close relations with the community where our happy lot is cast. Our committee work is so varied that there is no department of religious work adapted to young people which we cannot effectively compass. In the religious realm, the Society of Christian Endeavor, occupies exactly the same relative place that industrial training has in the new methods of education. This is a form of training which is not without reference to one's future employment. If men, for example, are to make a specialty of the applications of electricity, which now proves to have such a fascination for young men, besides the educational processes of the academy and of the college, they must in the shop have practical training, beginning at the rudiments.

In the recent course of addresses to students of Harvard College by gentlemen eminent in their respective professions, Mr. Charles Francis Adams, Jr., has advised young men to go into railroading simply to find power, as money and disciplined labor in such large measure are here concentrated. Now, in neither of these departments does simple instruction, received from others in ordinary schools suffice. One must, in acquiring an art, himself engage in its work. So is it in religious training. Here are acquisitions to be learned by experience and practice which neither a preacher nor a teacher can impart. As in surveying, facility is acquired in field practice. When this Second Cardinal Principle of our work was assigned to me, it was for a time thought best to call it Facility. It is acquired by the same means in religious work as it is in music.

It seems plain, from such a point of view as this, that providential elements are in the movement. It is precisely related to the great age-trend in the way that I have shown. This Society of Christian Endeavor is God's last experiment in Christian nurture. Nothing at hap-hazard has been introduced into it. With all deference to Mr. Clark, I have been accustomed to say that in that divine Sovereignty, whose right to elect agencies none of us can dispute, the founder of these societies was chosen to hold the die while, with the hammer, an Almighty hand administered the blow by which the form of this idea was struck out at a heat. If we were looking for further proof of this, we shall find it in the fact that while we, by experience, acquire some new facility in manifestation, yet no new principle has been superadded to the work since its beginning, neither has there been anything detracted without inevitable and noticeable harm and loss. Nor is there anything ephemeral in this idea, for while there is Christian work to do, for their own sakes, as well as for the sake of the work, the young must be trained to do it, and such schooling cannot begin at too early an age. But in the operations of our society, expression has a still more beneficent result. I have been showing that as bodily strength comes from its expenditure, and not from its hoarding; as the mental faculties gain through their using; as expression of thought in speech or writing increases one's treasure; as the memory, the affections, the imagination, gain in power by giving them exercise and by giving them play, so in our religious development expression is attended by an increment of power. But a man does not make himself strong merely for the sake of strength, but that his increased power may be of service; just as a man should not make himself rich for the mere sake of riches, but that he may use his wealth in beneficence and blessing. Strength, riches and capability of expression involve immense responsibilities to others. In the autumn of the year 1885, in a spot not remote from my place of residence, two boys were in jeopardy of their lives upon the water. One of them, gaining the shore, ran to a neighboring eminence to give the alarm and summon help. There he was seen by many engaging in violent gesticulations, which, not being understood, met with no response. He longed to save his companion, but alas, it was his misfortune, he was deaf and *dumb*. Yonder is all needful help, and at the foot of the hill a human being is perishing, and yet there stands in the midst an interested person, but tongue-tied and silent as the grave. Here, in an acted parable, is the church. Oh, this dumbness! Needy humanity, help in readiness, and the intercessor dumb! Oh! the affliction of it! To have children born dumb has always been accounted a misfortune by parents. So too, is it in the case of those who are born again. Dumbness among the children of God is an unmitigated calamity. Where there should be sounding out the living voice of testimony, spiritual life becomes so still, so quiet, that the church seems to be a vast aquarium. You look down upon living creatures that engage in various movements, but all is so voiceless! So-called Christians engage in varied activities, but the profoundest silence reigns. DUMB AS FISHES!! There is motion, but no utterance! Not only are they passing through life silently, but as Christians some of them, in that character, act as if they wanted to be unknown. Once, in Pisa, a company was pointed out as containing princes. No one was to know it. They were travelling *incog*. This is a method adopted, too, by many of the children of the Great King. They are princes of Royal Blood, but

prefer to be unknown.   They avoid, thus, all responsibility for keeping up to their princely character.   They are like the seven thousand
who had never bowed to Baal, of whom even Elijah did not know.
They are the Lord's hidden ones.   They have only witnessed up to
a negative point.   The best that could be said of them was that they
had never kissed Baal.   This negative testimony has at best but a
secondary value.   Sometimes in the discernment of this fact, the
children of this world are wiser in their generation than the children
of light.

So was it when a large commercial house sent out its travelling
salesman.   He seemed to possess all those qualities that would secure success.   He himself felt confident of ability ; but for some
reason that was alike a surprise to him and to the firm, he made only
unsuccessful journeys.   After thorough acquaintance with his methods, the senior member of the firm asked him into the counting room
to talk things over and in friendly fashion said : "We find that it
is your tendency on visiting a store to spend more or less time in be-
rating or deriding those business houses that are in direct competition
with us ; you labor to make it appear that such a competing house
has no standing in our own city, and this other one is trembling on the
uncertain verge of bankruptcy.   We find that you use your opportunity
in talking about them.   What we want is, when you have the ear of
your customer, that you should *talk about us.*   Talk about our credit
—our facilities for doing business—*Talk about us.*"   God is a great
business-doer.   In his name we are called to travel into all lands
and among all interests to represent him.   Much depends not only
upon expression, but as well upon the method of it.   We have no warrant and no occasion to antagonize anybody.   When we get the ear
of those to whom we are commissioned it is a supreme moment.   The
spirit of the Divine Firm of Business-Doers, the Father, the Son, the
Holy Ghost, is this : *Talk about us*—TALK ABOUT US.

A TIMELY MOVEMENT.

BY REV. C. A. DICKINSON, LOWELL.

The Young People's Society of Christian Endeavor is only five
years old, yet it has an aggregate membership of about fifty thousand.
The remarkable growth of the society, the kind reception which it
has uniformly met with among the churches, and its results in conversions and practical Christian work, all indicate that it is blessed of
God and destined to become a recognized and permanent institution
in the efficient church of the future.

The influence of the society has been neither divisive nor subver-
sive.   It has aroused few antagonisms, it has usurped no prerogatives.   The dominant desire of its friends has been to make it an

integral part of the church organization, and such it is generally regarded wherever it has been introduced. Some have perhaps thought that the single aim of the society is to make young people " talkative upon the subject of religion ; " and the query may have arisen, What advantage has it over the ordinary young people's prayer meeting ! To encourage Christian testimony is but a small part of the aim of the organization. Its work is larger than this, as Christian life in its fullness is larger than a mere Christian profession. The movement is timely, unique, and perhaps original in this, that an intelligent, systematic, cooperative effort is made to interest young people in the subject of personal religion, and train them up as efficient workers in the church.

It believes that the church should have a hand as well as a mouth, and that they both should be trained in youth. The society is the apprentice school to the active Christian life. It supplements the work of the Sunday school, and anticipates the work of the church, by teaching the young how to actualize Christian truth ; and thus it does for all the young people of the congregation what has ordinarily been done only for those who have been fortunate enough to have Christian parents and homes.

Adapting itself to the needs of the times, and to the special needs of the young, it endeavors to appropriate and sanctify such secular methods and principles as are evidently playing an important part in molding the rising generation.

The four cardinal ideas upon which the influence of the society seem to swing are suggested by the words, organization, expression, sociability, and obligation. There is nothing new in these ideas. They have been floating around in the consciousness of the Church for ages. They have been generally acknowledged as essential to the progress of Christ's kingdom. We believe, however, that they have never before been formulated into a working plan as we find them in the young people's society.

Despite the oft-uttered cry against " too much machinery in religious work," it is evident that without organization no great work can succeed in these busy days. A church, or a business, without wheels is a stone drag, well grounded, perhaps, but hardly fitted to bear the traffic of this nineteenth century. It is the aim of the society to find the minimum of organization which is consistent with the maximum of efficiency ; to provide the necessary wheels, but at the same time to have them properly adjusted to the living creature within.

Again, how to express the Christian life both orally and practically, is a question of vital importance. If the Congregational idea of the prayer meeting is to be realized in the future, if the church prayer meeting is not to lapse into a silent assembly, the gift of tongues must be sought for our young Christians. And if the future church is not to be a band of idlers, our young people must be taught that Christianity is love actualized in every form of humanitarian effort. By encouraging Christian testimony, and familiarizing the young with practical Christian worth, the society has already done invaluable service for the church.

The idea of sociability is also strongly emphasized, and a systematic effort made to give the social instinct and the pleasure instinct their legitimate place in the Christian life. Conceding that we ought not to expect mature experiences from young hearts, and recognizing the fact that many young people are repelled from the church because of its supposed censure of every form of amusement and pleasure, the friends of this movement have determined to face squarely the vexed question of " the church and amusements."

They do not presume to be able to solve it, but they hope, by entering into the sympathies of the young and recognizing some of their pleasure-loving propensities, to be able to convince them that, while religion is not frivolity, it certainly is not asceticism.

Above all, the idea of obligation is emphasized. With conscience on the one hand and the Lookout Committee on the other, the young Christian is reminded of his voluntary pledge to act well his part. If he be untrue to the monitor within, the monitor without stirs up his mind by way of remembrance, and thus the mildest kind of authority is made to supplement what might otherwise be a will too weak.

The pastors who have already entered heartily into this movement are surprised and delighted with the results. They find, coming up around them, a strong, active army of young Christians, who, without this organization, they are free to confess, would many of them have been, to-day, idle and indifferent members of their congregations.

The last report of the international committee of the Y. M. C. A. makes the startling assertion that seventy-five per cent. of the young men of this country are never seen inside of any church, that only fifteen per cent. of them can be called regular church-goers, and that but five per cent. are communicants. Now it is because the Young People's Society of Christian Endeavor has evidently sounded a halt to these drifting masses that we hail its advent with thankful hearts.

We say evidently, for the proof is before us. Since the appointment, last year, of a general secretary to oversee the work, there have been received at his office from thirty to fifty letters a day, inquiring concerning the work of the society, and testifying to its merits.

From the facts gathered in this way, it appears: (1) that the society has greatly increased the ratio of conversions in the churches where it has been introduced; (2) that, while it has done a great work among the children, its distinctive work in many of the churches has been to reach and interest the young men and women of the congregation; and (3) that the leading clergymen of nearly every large denomination in the land are giving the work their hearty indorsement. These points will probably be amply verified in the convention which meets at Saratoga this week, and which promises to be a worthy successor to the great June meetings in point of numbers and enthusiasm.

THE ELEMENT OF OBLIGATION.

BY REV. F. E. CLARK.

The element of *Obligation* is not only a most important and fundamental element in the work of the Society of Christian Endeavor; it is one that needs to be frequently and vigorously insisted on in all departments of religious life. In introducing this element and keeping it foremost in our work we have no easy task, for we are battling against a fallen and obstinate human nature. The World, the Flesh and the Devil combine to weaken this sense of obligation in religious matters, and we need at every point to buttress the resolutions of the new-born soul. The tendency of things is to sag. To counteract this sagging tendency in the religious life is one of the great designs of the Society of Christian Endeavor. The tendency of every tool is to grow dull. To keep the cutting dye of conscience sharp in some way is one of the great problems of the religious teacher. The weakness of the modern church lies along this line—the lack of any true and definite sense of obligation.

Many come into church membership, apparently with the impression that, since they have got aboard the gospel train, all they need do is to keep their seats (or berths in the sleeping car), show their tickets once in a while, proving by their certificates of church membership that they are in good and regular standing, and then relapse into a comatose state until they, with all the church, are drawn (by some other person's exertion) within the gates into the heavenly city. This is hardly a travesty on the way that many people settle down in the church, to be nothing and to do nothing. Their favorite hymn evidently is, "oh, to be nothing, nothing," and they answer their own prayer every day. The story of the minister's dream is true in ten thousand churches. He dreamed that he was harnessed to a heavy, lumbering hack, which it required all his exertion to move. At first things went nicely, for others were pulling with him, and still other friends were pushing behind; but, at length, it dragged heavily, the road grew sandy, the hills steeper; he put forth all his efforts and yet the chariot hardly seemed to move; when, just as with panting breath and steaming brow, he was about to give up in despair, he looked behind him, and behold! all who had been and who ought to be pulling and pushing had jumped in and were having a ride. The Deacons were looking out of the carriage window, the Superintendent of the S.´ S. was comfortably ensconced under the carriage robes, and all the young people of the church were hanging on behind. What we need is some power to lead all these people in the comfortable seats to feel their responsibility for the advancement of the gospel chariot, to lead them to be workers instead of passengers, pushers instead of hangers-on. To remedy this evil, especially among the young people, to make them not only workers, but to feel their individual responsibility for the work, was the Society\ of Christian Endeavor established; and it seeks to strengthen this feeling of responsibility by binding obligations *voluntarily assumed*.

To meet just this need and to strengthen this weak spot in human nature were the prayer-meeting rules devised, which read: "It is expected that all the members shall be present at every meeting, unless detained by some absolute necessity, and that each Active Member shall take some part, however slight, in every meeting. Once each month an Experience or Consecration meeting shall be held, at which each member shall speak concerning his progress in the Christian life. At each Experience or Consecration meeting the roll shall be called, and the response of the Active Members who are present shall be considered as a renewed expression of allegiance to Christ." These regulations which seem austere and iron clad to some, are really the vital characteristic of our work, and must never be lost out of view. The Society is capable of great flexibility of method, but this part of the prayer-meeting rule cannot be wisely altered or modified.

The organization can adapt itself to local needs as wide apart as Maine and Ceylon, but this rule should never be tampered with. Human nature is very much the same in the Sandwich Islands and in Saratoga. Young Tamil Christians and young Yankee Christians have the same enemies to fight within, however the foes without may differ, and in each one this sense of personal obligation must be cultivated and strengthened. We are not reasoning from theory alone, or from generalizations about human nature. Experience has been our teacher for the last five years, and it has been invariably found that those societies that have faithfully lived up to these binding obligations have flourished, while those that have not have partially failed.

There can be no true Society of Christian Endeavor that omits these prayer-meeting rules. Societies may differ in almost every other respect, they may have more or less committees, more or less duties assigned to each committee; the by-laws may vary widely, but these clauses which define the obligations of individuals to the work must remain substantially the same if the organization is to be a Society of Christian Endeavor. Let us briefly consider some of the characteristics of this obligation.

1. It should be *voluntarily assumed*. No one should be dragooned into becoming a member of the Society of Christian Endeavor. No one should be over-urged. In every church will be found a little band at least of the faithful and true. Confine the Active Membership to this band until others (as they surely will) see the advantage of this method of Christian work and *desire* freely to join in it. Great harm has often been done by crowding the ranks full of faint-hearted and half-convinced or wholly ignorant recruits who did not understand, and would not obey these obligations. Mr. Timorous, Mr. Faintheart, and Mr. Ready-to-Halt never helped Christians on in the

journey to the celestial city, and they never really helped themselves by pretending to go a little way with them.

When, however, these rules have once been intelligently adopted, let them be adhered to strictly, and enforced by every kindly and brotherly method. Let "absolute necessity" mean just the same thing in this connection that the word means elsewhere in the English language. It is amusing to call to mind how often the meaning of these plain words has been questioned. Do you wish to find out what they mean? Look in Webster's dictionary—they have the same meaning in our constitution. Of course, in the last result, the individual conscience must determine what coustitutes for it an "absolutely necessary" reason for staying away or for not participating in the meeting; but when the words are understood the conscience is tender, there will be little trouble on this score. An ordinary social engagement, a slight headache, an indisposition, the attraction of the evening newspaper or the last magazine, a cloudy sky, or a rain storm (to one in good health) will not be considered a valid excuse for neglecting a voluntarily assumed religious duty.

2. In the second place this obligation is *definite.* It is *for something.* The gun is not only loaded, it is aimed. When we fire at random into the sky we do not bring down many birds. Like Mr. Winkle in Pickwick Papers, we may by good luck bring down a bird and get a great reputation, even when we fire with one eye shut, but this is not often the case, and the reputation is not worth much.

The ultimate aim of this voluntary obligation, as our constitution states, is " to promote an earnest Christian life and make us more useful in the service of God ; " but as a means to the gaining of this great end, the obligation must be definite and tangible, directed toward particular duties which all can perform. This personal responsibility must be *for something.* The chief point is directed to the prayer-meeting, as has been already explained. But the committees embrace large numbers of the Society and being often changed, all the members sooner or later. For definite and specific and tangible amount and kind of work each committee is responsible, and the conscientious discharge of these obligations cannot but result in growth Godward.

Again, this sense of responsibility should not only be for *something,* but to *some one.* Again we need not remind all young Christians that they are primarily responsible to God. The Father above looks down, let us never forget that, and notes every secret thing. He knows our pledges, our excuses, our desires and aspirations. To Him we must render the final account, and from Him will come the final verdict, " Well done " or " Depart from me ! " But it is also necessary that to strengthen and keep awake this feeling of obligation, we should feel our responsibility to those around us—to our fellow Christians in the Society. For this reason the roll should be called every month that all may know who are the faithful ones. For this purpose the committees should each month have a written report to present to the Society, and that monthly business meeting, when the reports are presented, will be one of real spiritual power. The obligation for

serious work will be made definite and direct *to some one*. If the expedient of division bands, which has been found to work so well in
some places, is tried, let each individual be in a certain sense, responsible to the leader, and all the leaders to the pastor or president of the
society.

3. Again, let this obligation be *constant* and *regular*. One
great feature of our work is that this obligation for attendance upon
and participation in the meetings, comes regularly and definitely *every
week*. There are no long periods of inaction or sluggishness provided
for. There is no chance for the armor to grow rusty. Polish it *every
day* and it will surely keep bright. A consecration once a life time
or once a year will not answer ; let the commitment be renewed pub-
licly and openly to some from every day.

A great many non-church goers can give no better excuse for their
neglect of God's house than that they got into the habit of neglecting it.
They stayed away once, and it was easier to stay away the second
time, until at last it was more natural to stay than to go. Millions of
Christians have this same lame excuse for sluggishness and inactivity
—they got out of the way of working ; they began to neglect the
prayer-meetings, little by little, and to forget their duties until the
lapse of years has so incrusted them with callous indifference, that
they must be reconverted before they can do much for God.

The Society of Christian Endeavor proposes to provide no place for
such back sliders, nor do they wish to make the slide slippery and
easy for the unwary feet ; and so these prayer-meeting obligations and
the obligations of the committee work come as constantly and
regularly as the passage of time brings the successive weeks.

A young Christian cannot slip very far down hill before he finds
another landing place which arrests his sliding steps, and leads him
to ask whither he is tending.

4. Wherever there are rules there must be some provision for their
enforcement, otherwise they are not worth the paper on which they
are printed. The same principle that applies in our civil government in our schools and churches, must apply in our Societies. Since
we have rules there must be suitable and sufficient sanctions going
with those rules to make them of power. These sanctions are found
in the provisions for dropping members who are absent from three
consecutive consecration meetings without excuse.

This provision certainly cannot be considered harsh and unreason-
able. Such absence is *prima facie* evidence of an indifference to religious duties that is blame-worthy. It is a very easy thing to send
the reason of one's absence to the meeting if there is a good reason showing that the obligation was remembered. If one fails to do this for
three consecutive consecration meetings, the Lookout Committee
in the meantime having done what they can to win back the delinquent,
there is no reason for keeping such an Active Member in the Society.
The sooner he steps down and out, the better for the Society and for
all those influenced by him.

Of course, generous, brotherly kindness, and a true Christly spirit must be manifested, but it is to be hoped that this rule concerning the dismission of unfaithful members will never be modified. If it is, the societies will soon be filled with drones, useless and unfaithful members who only hinder the cause they have pledged themselves to help, and, worse than all, the sense of obligation of each member will be weakened. But if these rules are observed, if this definite and constant sense of obligation is maintained and above all if it is kept constantly in mind, as it surely will be under these conditions, that the primary obligation is to God for the building up of one's soul in spiritual graces, our Societies cannot fail to promote an earnest, Christian life among their members, and to make them more useful in the service of God.

MUSICAL CONTRIBUTION OF THE SOCIETY TO THE CHURCH WORK.

BY REV. S. W. ADRIANCE, LOWELL, MASS.

It may possibly seem presumptive to some of you that so early in our existence we should discuss so broad a topic as this. Yet it might be answered, where can it be better discussed than in the early dawn of our movement? This is just the time to get our bearings, to enquire what we are living for, to go round Jerusalem, marking her bulwarks, to see, perhaps, if the Christians have let any bulwark be neglected. Why not talk about our part in the branch of church work that relates to singing, or music in general? It is unnecessary for me to prove that singing has a great deal to do with progress in the churches. All the poetical and illustrative thoughts about the power of song I will refer you to hymnologists for. Let us straight to business.

1. It will be well if we understand that the shaping of the uses and style of music for the coming days is very largely in the power of the young. You are to say "what music shall be used for:" you are to determine whether we shall go on droning away music that will never convert; you are to say whether singing in connection with the Church shall be a reserved luxury or a great general demand. "Let every one that hath breath praise the Lord."

"The devil cannot stand music," said Luther. If Luther lived to-day, he would have to put in an adjective. The devil can stand any quantity of much music to-day. The devil has so largely obtained possession of musical instruments to-day, that a Christian parent almost dreads the thought of his boy learning to use the flute or violin, lest his life should sink to the dreary work of making the heels of this generation more developed than their heads or hearts. Now, one of two things must take place; either we are to part company with them and allow his dark majesty to own them, and

have the mark of the beast put on the brow of every one who takes
up a violin or cornet, or else we are to have consecrated young people to arise who shall take them up and, in the name of Christ, keep
them from vile associations and uses. Why isn't the latter feasible?
Look at the bands that pass along the street. How many of the per-
formers are young men? And if your Active Member of your Society of Christian Endeavor joins a band or orchestra, why do you almost
know that most of his work will be done in ranks or theatres or ball
rooms? We are not ready to part with these instruments; our young
people must come out and be separate. Consecrate this to higher
uses; form orchestras right out from our members, and have every
violin anointed with the blood of Christ, to be used to accompany
and assist the sacred song.

So, too, in singing there is this remedial work to be done. I was
looking through a large music store the other day for a baritone solo,
and found it hard to escape from the languishing invitations of love-
song after love-song. It is too bad that even in the musical sociables
of our Y. P. S. C. E. our young people should be compelled to
express their fondest hopes in languishing love-songs. The Christian life of many of our young people does need toning up on the
subject of secular music, before very much can be done toward Christian music. The reform in music must come through the high stand
of young people. I wonder if our young men and women are not
willing to stand by their religious convictions in the matter of song.
A generation of Christian Endeavor effort would do a great deal
toward it. I imagine that the tone of society in many a village is decided by the Y. P. S. C. E. in that village.

2. Looking at actual things, we have a hint of something definite
in what has already been done. Only a little, perhaps, but enough
to point out the way, though it is merely the blaze on a tree.

a. These societies have increased the responsiveness of congregational singing. It is noteworthy that their prayer-meetings and their
more earnest Christian life has made them more ready to sing as if
it were bidden them of God to do so, as indeed it is. May I say
that there is an especial work for societies in villages and small
country corners in this line. It is said that Orpheus could charm
even the rocks by his singing. But it would be difficult to imagine the droning, sleepy singing of many of our country church
services charming the stones which take the place of hearts there
No service can be so effctually regenerated as through its bright earnest hearty singing. Whether you have your formal choir or no, I
appeal to you, young Christians, never to think idly of the hymn-
singing in the Sabbath service. We have done that already too
much. It is time to rout that heresy hip and thigh with great
slaughter, and make our Sabbath service ring with its anthems to
God. Let me tell you of an ideal musical service. I take its descrip-
tion from a very old book called the Old Testament; "It came even
to pass, when the trumpeters and singers were as one, to make one
sound to be heard in praising and thanking the Lord; and when they

lifted up their voice with the cymbals and trumpets and instruments of music, and praised the Lord, saying for He is good, for His mercy endureth forever: that then the house was filled with a cloud, even the house of the Lord, so that the priest could not stand to minister by reason of the cloud; for the glory of the Lord filled the house." 2 Chron. 5:13–14.

We are glad that in many quarters this result has followed the formation of these societies. Close to this is the increased power of song in the regular Church prayer-meeting, as well as the earnest singing of the Endeavor prayer-meeting.

b. These societies have already done something toward the greater effectiveness of the Sabbath school. Some of them have indeed, a musical committee, and the choir which leads the singing at the Sabbath school is composed of members of the Y. P. S. C. E.

c. The importance of the society in the general Church work of villages can hardly be estimated. There the control of the singing is practically in their hands. But one effect among the many which might take place has taken place. The desire more heartily to be of use in this part of the Gospel work, has led the members, of one society at least, to gather together once a week in the careful drill over some fine rendering of Haydn or Handel. The result of this cannot fail of being permanently useful to the cause of Christ.

d. But perhaps the most effective work already done, is in another direction. We have but just entered upon this. It is in connection with the Sabbath evening service. This new movement of Evangelistic Service for Sabbath evening, is yet hardly begun. The cases in which it has been tried prove beyond a doubt that it is to become a wonderful lever in prying the people out of their indifference. Now, our Young People's Societies seem destined, if they are willing to enter this field of their destiny, to be a powerful ally to the Church—or rather a powerful factor in the Church toward making this evening service of vast influence. And the best of it is that this is just as applicable to our villages, however small, as to our cities. Nowhere will an extra service of song bring out such a crowded house as in the country. There is no doubt but that, if the Young People's Society in the country would take special hold of the evening service, offer their help to the pastor, promising him that they will each Sabbath evening or every other Sabbath evening, assume charge of the music of the evening serv ce, and have a goodly chorus on hand, there is no doubt, I say, that that service will call out large audiences. It is a very grave mistake to suppose that the People's gospel service is a city plant which will not flourish in the country soil. I speak not out of theory but of practice. It was at one time my pleasure to drill the members of my Society in such work, and the large audiences which came, proved beyond a doubt the reserve power in every society to do this. The thorough organization, the *esprit de corps*, and above all the earnest desire for the prosperity of the Church which has been developed by these societies, offer an already prepared basis for such work. But to facts. I know of a city Church, where the ex-

periment of making the evening service full of power has been tried
with poor success for years. There were many difficulties in the
way; but though this Church possessed the finest of quartettes, there
was not power, heart-power, enough in such artistic singing, to call
out even an average congregation. At length from the Young People's Society a large chorus choir was formed. The quartettes acted
with it. The Y. P. S. C. E. took that evening service under its responsibility, saw to the printing of posters announcing the pastor's
subject, and the result was the complete filling of the church; so that
one of the oldest deacons of the church told me they were able to do
what had never been done before, have a large evening attendance.
In another the quartette has been discarded, and the singing is lead
by the large chorus choir of which the Y. P. S. C. E. is the real pro-
vider. These are hints; they show what unmined resources there
are with you to vastly increase the attractive power of the Church over
the public. Are you willing to set yourselves to this work? I wish
it might be definitely taken hold of by the many societies of villages
here. Talk it over with your pastor. I should be glad with these
other brethren to formulate some general schedule of such Sabbath
Evening Services, adapted especially.for villages, for the 'three winter months of December, January and February.

(Since I made this statement to the Conference, information has
been given of the same result in several instances, and also of orchestras formed in the Y. P. S. C. E. to accompany the singing.)

e. Growing out of this, the thorough organization of our societies
has presented a favorable opportunity of meeting at suitable times for
the practice of choral singing, a thing which has already occurred in
various places.

3. So much for what has been done. These are of course only
hints, they simply show what may still be achieved. Now comes the
question, how far will you set yourselves toward the future? It is evident, I think, that the power of song in bringing the lost world to
Christ is hardly in its A, B, C, yet.

a. There is something to be expected in the way of finer singing.

b. Something too is to be desired in exercising an exclusive power. There is a sickening use of great gifts in singing to nonsense, and
low sentiment. Miss Havergal has a sound chapter in one of her
books on the consecrated use of the voice. Now, you are here, to
regenerate the world, I rejoice that I am speaking to young people,
who are ready to make earnest endeavors for Christ. Have you consecrated your voice to Christ? Have you consecrated the hand that
plays the violin, the breath that brings music from the cornet, the
fingers that know the secrets of the ivory keys of piano and organ?
Shall not the Lord get from among you many a Sankey, or Bliss, to
sing lost men into Paradise? Are there not to be prepared from some of
these Societies male quartettes, double quartettes, like the Ruggles
quartette of Boston? Are there not materials in your midst, furnish-
ing pleasure and grand drill, for orchestras, whose training shall
never be reduced to the miserable assistance of the devil's worth; I

do not know why it is preposterous to imagine a consecrated orchestra, every member a disciple of Christ. Let our Home Missionary Society have a quartette and a little orchestra, all Christians, to go on a gospel music campaign through such a State as Montana, and nothing will so prick the bubble of that coarse Western infidel conceit as that.

Are there not young ladies who are to be Christian soloists? Are there not young men to be precentors in these days of Congregational Singing?

c. Perhaps you will think this paper visionary, but there occur to me as I write such possibilities untouched as yet, of the new use of song for Christ, in the redemption of the word, that I am going to free my mind. Last summer, I was invited in Lowell, to speak on one of our commons. I was assured that there would be singing, there was, but I was ashamed to be caught backed up by such singing. Yet they listened to it. Thoughts would be busy. If this rabble will be quiet during this singing, what power would there be if it were better. The fault of our out-of-door services in cities is their weakness. It is sad that we Christian people palm off in such out-door meetings a thin, extemporized service, which ought to bring us into disgrace with the crowds. Why verily, if a band should play on the common, as we Christian people sing, they would be hooted from the green. A thoroughly organized chorus of twenty voices backed by a brief sermon of fifteen minutes would bring many a person into the churches to hear more of such music. Pray, is it not a reasonable thought that many a Society of Christian Endeavor can do this?

d. It seems to me, again, that the Society of Christian Endeavor has something to contribute toward the church work by a decision in respect to the Hyms which the churches are to sing. Unintentionally, unconsciously, but all the more effectively you are to revise the Hymn books. The Hymn books which the earnest, active Christian efforts need, will have, will make, will be devotional. Such tried Hymns as "My Faith looks up to Thee," "More Love, O Christ, to Thee," "Jesus, keep me near the Cross," will stand. Hymns will be more Christlike. They will be more aggressive. Any one who examines the Hymns you want to sing, will discover the frequent use of the soldier Hymns, "Stand up, stand up for Jesus," "We're marching to Canaan with banner and song," Then again, unless I misapprehend, the large constituency which is embracing Christian Endeavor principles, desire spirited Hymns. The droning of minor refrains does not suit. And lastly, the demand will be for more evangelistic Hymns, for invitations, songs of grace, etc., etc. This brings me to the Gospel Hymns. It is the fashion to decry them, but this is a course which hurts most him who tries it. Decidedly, the movement is in favor of the better class of these Hymns. There cannot be published to day, a Prayer-meeting Hymn book, to be successful, which does not draw largely from them. Even conservative Dr. Robinson, in his book, "Spiritual Songs," for church and choir, makes large drafts on this book.

And it may be, that we may be able to prepare an earnest, aggressive Hymn book, by selection from the old and new.

THE DESIRABILITY OF CONFERENCES, STATE AND LOCAL.

BY REV. RALPH W. BROKAW, BELLEVILLE, N. J.

If I may be allowed to tamper a little with the wording of my theme, I will change it slightly, so that it will read, "The Desirability of Conferences, State OR Local," instead of "State AND Local." The practical question before us, then, is—"Are such assemblies profitable; and, if so, why?" We answer, YES, and for the following reasons, viz. :

1. *Because many of our members, on account of distance or expense, cannot attend the General Conference.* And for them, to a certain extent at least, these local gatherings may take its place. Of course they will not afford so rich a feast of reason and so gracious a flow of soul as does a concourse like this. Nevertheless, the same outcome *in kind*, if not in *degree*, they ought to effect. For do not all conventions produce certain things in common? Just as there is here created a spiritual magnetism whose subtle force is manifested all along the line of this loving labor for the young, in increased knowledge of the work, in deepened affection for the workers, in quickened interest and in enkindled enthusiasm; so there will be, for the same causes, similar results from local conferences. This yearly pilgrimage to a shifting Y. P. S. C. E. Mecca, like the journeys of the weak and weary to the springs of Saratoga, is the lively source of health and vigor to hundreds of individual organizations far and near. I venture to say that no one who has had the experience of being in such a gathering as this questions its desirability for a single instant. And if this is good, so may those for which I plead be *also good.* I take it for granted, then, that you all respond to what I have thus far said with a hearty Amen. But this is general. I pass on now to more specific considerations.

2. Local conferences are desirable as *distributors* of information and influence from headquarters. In no other way can facts and fire be so well disseminated. It is true that the printed page can and *does* accomplish a useful service to this end. So far in our history, we have been compelled to rely largely upon this instrumentality in instructing those who have been anxious to learn about our methods of work. But it cannot be compared for effectiveness with the living voice and personal presence of those who speak what they do know and testify to that which they have seen. After men have read the best pamphlets we can prepare, they yet want to talk with some one whose knowledge is based on experience. Consequently some of us have to make many public addresses, even in the wake of a small deluge of press work. Then, too, public speech reaches those (and

they are not a few, I assure you) who habitually consign circulars to
the waste-basket, and that other equally large class who, apparently,
would rather remain ignorant than to carefully peruse elaborate ex-
planations in printers' ink. Wherefore the utility of the kind of conferences named in the subject. The mighty engine running day and
night in its solitary place in the city generates the electricity, but it
does not distribute it. These beautiful clusters of lights, whose radi-
ant beams flood the distant parks or illumine scores of streets, are
connected by wire channels with the single source of their power.
Without these means of distribution the engine's energy would be
almost wasted. So, it seems to me, without running the parable
" on all fours," are the local conferences to the General Conference.
We want the light of what we learn, or what we are made to feel,
or what we are inspired to work for, by the engine of this enthusiastic and uplifting meeting, to shine on thousands of communities.
We desire that all the young people in this rapidly growing society
shall share with us the benefits of our coming together. We are
anxious that they shall become acquainted with whatever good and
helpful things are brought forth here. In what better way can we
accomplish this than by gathering in conference the societies located
in the single states, or within convenient distance from each other,
and letting discreet and earnest men act as connecting agents, *thus* to
distribute enlightening and encouraging forces? Surely there is none.

3. Again, such conferences are desirable as *advertisers.* Do not
quarrel with me for using this word, so unpleasantly associated with
quackery, circuses, and the man who can tell you how to raise a
moustache on the most unpromising soil. I know of no other that
expresses the idea as well. We believe thoroughly that we have a
good institution in this Society of Christian Endeavor. It meets a
demand. It is the outcome of a legion of experiments. It is the
crystallization of he wisdom of many. It works well. Is it not
proper, therefore, that we should publish our success to the outside
church world? Nay, more, is it not our *duty?* And, if so, we are
justified in devising legitimate ways for advertising ourselves to our
Christian brethren. Now a local or state conference does just this precisely. It is announced beforehand. Curiosity is excited in the minds
of the uninitiated to find out what this society is. A cordial invitation
is extended to the public to attend the sessions. Many accept it.
They hear descriptions of the character of the movement; listen to
lively discussions of methods; look upon the earnestness manifested;
and are convinced that such an organization would be a good one to
establish in their own church. It is not long before a new society is
added to the roll. Beside, the omnipresent newspaper reporters are
on hand to see and hear. They publish our proceedings, and the
result is, that everybody around receives an introduction to us. I am
confident that the Connecticut State Conference, held last November
in New Haven, was an advantage in this way, as well as in many
others. In fact, did not a prominent minister in that college town
declare, after attending that splendid meeting, that he was deter-

mined to start a Society of Christian Endeavor in his own church? Doubtless he did so. At all events let it be remembered that BEFORE that conference Connecticut *had less than 20 societies,* and NOW has OVER 70. I tell you, such conferences pay. Did I say it was a splendid meeting? So it was. Indeed, a fitting exclamation would have been: If this is only a State Conference, if such zeal for the Master burns within these narrow limits, what must a General Conference be! How vigorous must be this new servant of the church for the spiritual training and development of the young!

4. These local conferences may be useful in *arresting* and *answering* the thousand and one minor questions, which, as our present overcharged program proves, the General Conference has not time to consider, and which it has outgrown. They should act like the lower civil courts in stopping and dealing finally with smaller things. Then, too, the varying local circumstances and conditions give rise to important matters which would be out of place here. A suburban population, like ours in the vicinity of the metropolis for example, has to be taken care of in a different way from that employed to reach those who live in self-centered towns or cities, or in the outlying districts. The little state of Connecticut and the little bigger state of New Jersey present somewhat different phases of church life and character which need special provision. This can be obtained through state gatherings better than through any other channel now existing.

5. Once more, these conferences are desirable for the *cultivation of neighborliness and fraternity* among those of the same sections of country. They have the same effect as union services, viz.: to minify our ecclesiastical differences, and to magnify our ecclesiastical and spiritual resemblances. By them the ties which bind our hearts together in Christ are strengthened. Can we overestimate this element of power? Can we afford to lose sight of it, or fail to employ it in this work? Our Saviour's prayer, "that we may all be one," we are bound to remember and answer as nearly as possible. It might be a good thing to adopt, as one of our mottoes, the legend on the Dutch coat of arms, viz.: "Een-dracht maakt macht"—in union is strength. Were I not in the Reformed (Dutch) Church, modesty would not stand in the way of my suggesting it. Is it not exceedingly profitable for brethren in the Lord to become acquainted with each other, to see eye to eye, to join in prayer and praise and counsel? The seventy thought so when they returned from the fulfillment of their special mission. The Apostles thought so, for when they were come and had gathered the church together at Antioch, they rehearsed all that God had done with them, and how he had " opened a door of faith unto the Gentiles." Scholars think so, for summer schools of languages, science and philosophy are the order of the day. The church thinks so, else why church congresses, and pan-Presbyterian councils, and pan-Episcopalian convocations? Politicians think so, for their work is organized after this fashion in every state in the Union. Therefore, for these and other reasons, let the

recommendation of last year be reaffirmed by this assembly, and let it be carried out as far as practicable in the various states where we have a following.   In the place of anniversaries of single societies, would it not, in many instances, be much better to combine energy and ability in a local conference?   Do not misunderstand me.   Individual celebrations of society birthdays are fitting.   If the thing aimed at is a morning or evening service merely, in which the pastor's sermon shall be in the line of our work, all well and good. But if they are forced to take on the form of a conference, with papers, discussions, a visit and address from the General Secretary, and perhaps speeches from others also, they are very likely to make but little impression upon the church community where they are held.   There is not range enough to them.   There is in them but little chance for interchange of views.   There is no accumulation of experience or wisdom.   And beside, if each society asks for the presence of the General Secretary, or other willing workers among the officers of the United Society, and if they respond, they will have but little time to attend to the particular duties devolving upon them. Our Secretary, being in the greatest demand, of course, I am afraid would soon have to be sent on a vacation to Europe for rest and recuperation.   Did you ever stop to think how long it would take to kill the most vigorous man who, working all day in his office, spends his nights in public speaking and travelling?   Not long, I assure you. And if he must reach all whom he ought to reach through anniversaries, we shall soon be compelled to elect a new person for this place.   Whereas, under far more favorable conditions, by less expense and exposure, and with better speakers, through *local conferences* HE can wield a wider and more satisfactory influence.   Moreover, you will have livelier, healthier and happier gatherings.   They will give a new impetus to the societies composing them, and attract very much more outside attention.   So *consolidate* where you can. Call upon every member to do his share of the work.   When a man enters into any human association, he is expected to take an intelligent interest in its work, to maintain its honor, and to further its weal.   There is no reason why less should be expected of members of the Society of Christian Endeavor.   Indeed, they have already pledged it.   The very name of their organization will be a reproach to them without it.   The time is past when Christians, old or young, can thrive and glorify the Master by munching theological or ecclesiastical confectionery.   We must "awake and put on our strength." It is easy to go with the multitude, it is delightful to be relieved of every duty but the pleasant one of passing criticism on other people. But this is utterly wrong.   There is more *now* to be done than there ever was.   To be sure, the foundation is laid.   That we cannot touch.   Yet every wall of the sanctuary is to be heightened.   This work in behalf of the rising generation is one of these walls.   And this we have only just begun.   What "room there is for enlargement, for improvement, for increase of hospitality, for growth in all noblest knowledge and sympathy!   And so far as the *entire* church is concerned"—a part of which we certainly are—"what an opportunity there is for her to-day to stand outside of her own walls of salvation, and say to the sons of men: ‘This is your Father's house, and in it there is bread enough, and to spare!’" "The church," says another, "includes all other houses that *are* good, or want *to be* good. What is the church to *our* imagination? Is it only one great central meeting-place? But that will not suffice. Round about there must be many little houses—outer dependencies having direct connection with the house-fire and with the house-comfort; so near that the voice of prayer can be overheard; so near, indeed, that now and again some gentle tone of strong appeal can penetrate." Is not our position such in relation to the church? If so, my friends, let us keep ourselves THERE, and never in our conferences attempt to assume prerogatives which do not belong to us. The rather, as *hands or even feet,* obedient to the command of our head, be it ours to serve God and our fellows, *through the church,* in a manner calculated to call forth her approbation and insure her affection. Thus shall we glorify our Master in most wise as well as most Christian *Endeavor.*

> " Crowns and thrones may perish,
>   Kingdoms rise and wane,
> But the Church of Jesus
>   Constant will remain;
> Gates of Hell can never
>   'Gainst that church prevail—
> We have Christ's own promise,
>   And that cannot fail.
> Onward, Christian soldiers,
>   Marching as to war,
> With the cross of Jesus
>   Going on before.

(S. Baring Gould.)

ASSOCIATE MEMBERSHIP.

The Rev. H. C. Hitchcock of Somerville, Mass., opened the discussion of the next topic, namely, that of "Associate Membership." The following is an abstract of Mr. Hitchcock's remarks. He began by saying :

A great deal of valuable work has been gone through with this forenoon, and the hour is late for commencing on a new theme. For the part that is expected of me, however, I shall not need to detain you long. Indeed, it ought not to require many words to convince any one at all familiar with the work in which we are engaged, of the importance of that which is really its one distinguishing feature, and which makes it unlike any previous organization for the religious development of the young, namely, the provision of our constitution for an Associate Membership. This, it seems to me, is the one master-stroke of genius, and I may almost say of inspiration, in this whole affair ; the fact that while it is an avowedly religious organization, it has a place, and a warm place, for those who are not religious, but whom our faith proposes before long to make religious. The more I think of it, the more I see in this arrangement an immense potency of fresh life for our churches, an immense and evergrowing power for drawing the young people of our congregations nearer to us, getting them more directly under our influence, and bringing them eventually within the sacred fold of the christian covenant itself. Possibly you will say I am over-enthusiastic on this point. But let me explain why this was the one feature that first arrested my attention, and saved me, very likely, from tossing the whole scheme into the waste-paper basket, as we are apt to do with so many of the novelties that come flying to us on every wind. The simple fact was, that when this Christian Endeavor plan happened along my way, it found me very hungry for advice in a certain line. It found me borne down with anxiety for certain young people in my own congregation ; and what pastor has not felt this kind of anxiety? It found me studying literally night and day on the question what to do for young people who had reached that "critical age" about which we hear so much, when it is very important to keep a hand on them, but when also it requires the best wisdom to approach them with direct religious effect; young people who are not ready yet to come to you for direct religious inquiry, but who, nevertheless, have their own deep thoughts, as all young people have ; who know their duty to God, know they have souls to be saved, and who, as you feel, must somehow be laid hold of and brought into the ark of safety before they shall go forth from their student days into the busy whirl of life. What pastor, I say, has not felt this kind of a load heavy upon him? I had a desire to increase my opportunities with these young people, to see them oftener, to get myself nearer to them, and them nearer to me ; and to do this in a way not to frustrate my ultimate end, which was to make christians of them. Awkward work would not answer, for here were bright minds and keen sensibilities, already well along in school and some in college ; minds, therefore, with whom the thing must be done skillfully or else it were far better left undone. I had thought of several things ; first, of a social club, then of a reading circle, and still again of an old fashioned debating society ; anxious to get hold of some instrumentality, but not likely either of these, for the great reason that, though an association of that pattern might draw the young people together, it would not be a distinctly religious organization, and religion, if brought in at all, would seem lugged in. What gain would it be, after all, for me to organize my young people into a society where literature or entertainment should be looked upon as the main thing, and religion only a formality with which to dignify an opening or closing moment? Would it not be like going a long way around Robin Hood's barn to reach the end of my journey? So, I say, I was tugging at the problem. To get something social and attractive, and at the same time christian and spiritual, was what I wanted and wanted right away, but how to get it was the question. I was in the woods, in short, a good deal lost, and wandering vaguely when the idea of this Society found me and showed me the way out. I shall never forget the relief that the discovery of this *associate* feature brought to me. I was not two minutes in deciding, after reading Bro. Clark's little primer of a constitution that a club, or a reading circle, or a debating society, was not the thing for my young people just then, but that the "Christian Endeavor" was the thing. Here, to begin with, was a mode of organization that would be distinctly religious; offering social and other possible attractions, to be sure, but all under the canopy of Christ; a place in which the most earnest and even pointed spiritual counsel would never seem out of place, but where those entering would expressly offer themselves as fair subjects for that kind of labor. And yet, while it would be positively Christian, its religiousness would be equalled by its hospitality and by the cosmopolitan and Christly breadth with which it would open its door and extend its arms of welcome, so that every well-meaning young person would be only glad to enter its portal and to conform to its regulations. Here, first of all, and best of all, would be a prayer meeting, where unconverted young people would receive an impression every week from the worship of their Christian young friends. That impression would surely tell, for nothing in all the world would so affect young hearts as the confessed divine experience of other young hearts. And so by the steady pull of sympathy and faith, emphasized by the might of the spirit, the renewing work of God could not fail to be done. I was not long, I say, in resolving what to do; and the result among us in our Day St. Society of Somerville, has been more satisfactory than I could find words to describe to you in the few moments that remain to me to-day. I will only say this, that I should condemn myself as an ungrateful minister, as an ungrateful man, if I did not bring my hearty tribute of honor to this noble invention, this Heaven-inspired thought of Christian Endeavor, which has helped so many pastors and churches in their work already, and which, in my judgment, is destined in the days to come to fill the whole earth with its triumphs.

Mr. Hitchcock then referred to the great responsibility involved in this feature of Associate Membership, the many practical difficulties arising out of it, and proposed to answer a few of the more common inquiries that are suggested by the experience of young societies in this regard. He urged these four points:

First of all, treat your Associate Members with cordiality. Your very first business with each newly arrived member is to convince him that he never got into a better place than when he joined your society; a place where he was more kindly treated, or found better friends. If you have one Associate Member who does not feel so, then your work is a failure at the very start as far as he is concerned. The best workers in a society are those who are on hand early at the prayer-meeting. The moments before and after meeting are very important for putting the underpinning beneath your spiritual edifice.

Be on the look-out for the members as they come to the meeting. Go out and meet that young man who was elected only last week. Lock arms with him while the bell is still tolling. Take a few steps with him along the side-walk; have a nice little friendly talk. If the heart of Christ and the motive of Christ be in you, you will make him feel it, and you will gain a place in his heart, Take him into the meeting with you; find him a seat by your side; hand him a hymn-book; show him the scripture lesson, and so in these little ways prove to him that you think of his comfort and are bound to have him feel at home. And then if you shall arise in that meeting to pray, there will be one heart ready to have some faith in your prayer. A few minutes are enough to make your neighbor look upon you as a good fellow and as somewhat fit for the kingdom of Heaven; and a few minutes are also enough to leave him in serious doubt about it. Remember that right here your work begins, and certain it is that it can never go forward till it begins. Right here in these social and friendly offices towards your Associate Members, you are to lay the first foundations for that after work in them which you hope to see accomplished.

Then secondly, insist upon order in your meetings. Require every member, both Active and Associate, to respect you, to respect himself, and to respect the Heavenly King, so far as never to forget that a religious meeting is not the place for any kind of trifling. Have a president who is not afraid of any young man or young woman, and who will know how to make his authority felt if necessary. In nearly all cases a word kindly spoken will be sufficient to check any indecorum. But some of our societies in their rapid growth, have received into Associate Membership a large number of youngerly boys and girls, in some of whom it may be that the sentiment of reverence has been only imperfectly developed. You are glad to have them come, and you want to keep every one of them. But if you do keep them, you find that, besides the work of religion, you have assumed also a work of education; and a very useful work it will be, provided you only do it. First of all, as I said before, treat them with cordiality, make them your friends and put about them the restraints of love; but in any case tolerate no disorder. Any incorrigible disturber should not be allowed to remain. I have heard of one or two societies that had been brought into sore straits, and that were even on the border of dissolution, from a lack of sympathy between the Active and Associate elements. Such a society probably needs at once a few older and wiser and firmer hands to take the control of it. Very likely the pastor ought to lend a hand; or, call a private meeting of the better and more serious members, Associate as well as Active, ask them to take hold of the matter, to speak personally with the persons at fault, appealing to their better nature, and in this way a reformation would probably be secured. But certain it is in such a case that something must be done, and done promptly. As it is, your coming together will be productive of more harm than good. At all hazards, the Christian element must rule, and must never allow itself to be oversloughed. For, remember your Society is yours; yours for the sake of Christ, yours for the loftiest and most sacred uses, and no mortal under the sky must be allowed to destroy it. Hence, I would never give up and say, Disband your society; but rather, purge it if necessary, that it may bring forth fruit. This, however, only in passing, and with reference to those few cases of embarrassment about which some inquiry has been made.

My third point is, that you owe it to your Associate Members to have a good prayer-meeting. All clouds of difficulty will vanish from your sky if you are able to have a good prayer-meeting. Let your Active Members do their duty; let them offer themselves bravely, devoutly, loyally, as the organ and mouth-piece of the Holy Ghost, and your society will not fail to command the respect, and ere long the gratitude, of your Associate Members. To this end, your Prayer-Meeting Committee will have something to do. It must not only provide a leader for the prayer-meeting, but, what is no less important, it must provide a following for the leader. Your leader may be a green hand, and sometimes must be, for every leader must have a first time; but give him a good following, and you will still have a prayer-meeting. Look out for your following. The first minute, after the leader, will often make or kill the meeting. A gap of silence in a prayer-meeting may do well enough, provided it is appointed and called for, and is truly worshipful; but if it be only a token of the cowardice and irresolution of Christians, waiting for somebody *else* to take part, it is the devil's opportunity. I have seen an unconverted person nominate a hymn to be sung, in sheer pity for the weakling professors who were suffering the time to pass in distressing silence. That was simply dreadful. Two or three christians could better offer themselves to be crucified, rather than allow such a thing as that to happen. Aim at a good deal of prayer in your meetings, and not too much singing. Dr. Nettleton was sometimes afraid that the people would sing the Holy Ghost out of a meeting faster than they prayed Him in. But a plenty of the right kind of prayer will keep the singing also prayerful. In my society, when we were new and when there were not any too many to take part, we found it useful to form a praying band within the society of those who would agree to pray in every meeting, and to be the *first* to pray if possible. This little device brought a marked change into the tone of our meetings. Let the chairman of the prayer-meeting committee, for example, organize such a praying band, keeping a list of their names, and adding to his list as fast as he can find members who will thus pledge themselves. In this way even a young society may soon have working force enough to make a strong prayer-meeting.

But finally, and above all else, it is the *conversion* of your Associate Members that you are aiming at. And because this is your great end, as I have said before, you must teach your hearts really to love them; to love them in a real christian way; to love them, not because they are comely or attractive personally, not because they wear good clothes, not because they come from good families, but because they belong to the Lord Christ; because he loves them and desires that they should discover and behold his love for them, and because, further, He has appointed that you, even you, should help them to the discovery, that you should tell them the story, that your prayer for them, your human sympathy and interest and friendship shall image to them the dear heart of Christ, and so by the blessing and power of his Word and Spirit speaking through you, to open their hearts to this wondrous and saving disclosure. How is it? What are we here for? Mr. President, what means this Conference after all? What are we going to take away with us? Is not this the very heart and core of the whole matter? My brother, my sister, whosoever you are, and whencesoever you come, are you a member of one of these societies? Do you call yourself a Christian, an Active Member? Let us have a word of self-examination before we go. What are you aiming at by your membership in these societies? Is it simply fun, social enjoyment, to meet your friends and to have a good time? You an Active Member, and is this all your membership means? Then I say that your heart is stone-blind to the higher joy and blessedness which lie at your very door. Why, look at it. What an opportunity is here. Fifteen thousand Associate Members! Did not our hearts leap in glad surprise when our Secretary read us his footing the other day? Forty-five thousand Active, and fifteen thousand Associate Members represented in this convention to-day! In the name of Christ, I say to you, these FIFTEEN THOUSAND are your field. Has He not given them to you. Has He not brought them to you? Has He not placed them, as it were, in the very hollow of your hand? Have they not verily come to you of their own accord? Have they not, by their own free act, committed their souls to your keeping and your influence, asking you to pray for their eternal safety? What fairer field could you ask? These choicest youth of the land! These brightest, and noblest, and most promising of our congregations and our communities! If you have no heart or faith for such an opportunity as this, when, I ask, are you ever going to do anything for the Redeemer's cause? God help us, that when another Conference shall meet, one year from to-day, we may hear the glad report that all of the Fifteen Thousand, and more, too, have been gathered in.

GENERAL SECRETARY'S REPORT.

In the opening lines of the Secretary's report, read at Lowell in October, 1884, we find the following: " The report which is now submitted to you might be condensed into one word, ' Progress.' It is gratifying to know that our plan is rapidly working its way into favor and that it is destined at no very distant day to be a very important factor in the evangelization of the world."

In a paper read before the last annual conference at Old Orchard, the Rev. Mr. Clark, in speaking of the needs of the society, said: " We have apparently reached the limit of effort under the present system. God, as we believe, has put this labor upon us. He has brought us to a point where we must either advance or stand still, and standing still really means a retreat." In the address made a few months ago by the trustees, in introducing the work of the United Society we find this statement: " It is confidently expected that there will be a movement this winter all along the line." So much for the prophecies of our friends in the past. To-day you are to learn whether these gentlemen are entitled not only to your love and esteem, but also to your admiration, as men who could see into the future and could plan for the performing of that problem which upon examination we find presented itself soon after the last conference, aye before that time. To-day my repert to you is made, as you know, in connection with the office of secretary of the U. S. C. E. You all know what led to the formation of that society. It had for an aim the furtherance of the work of Christian Endeavor to an extent which it would be impossible to reach, without the application of time and money to the undertaking. The experiment, if such you choose to call it, has been tried and the results have reached far beyond the expectation of the most sanguine. To refer again to the quotation made above, we can still claim " progress " as our report to-day, and better still, we may add to that watchword the encouraging cry " advancement," while thanks to the wisdom and kind assistance of friends of the cause, we can look back to that point at which we found ourselves last year and realize that under God's help we were enabled neither to retreat nor to lose any of the advantage gained in the past. On the other hand, marshalling our forces into more compact and methodical order, we were allowed to go forward and fulfilling the hope of our trustees, to aid in a most decided movement all along the line. Taking for our field our whole country, and stretching our line of battle from Maine to California. Better than all that; better than the fulfillment of our past numerical record; better than the spread of the work into new fields; better than the fact that day by day the public is coming to realize the force of, and to give a place to, the cause of Christian Endeavor. Better than all this, is the pleasure and the joy which must be ours when we realize that the last part of Mr. Stephenson's prophecy is coming plainly to the front, and that the Society of Christian Endeavor is already recognized throughout our land, and even in other lands, as an important and successful feature in the great work of evangelizing the world, particularly that most important and influential part, the young people. Though founded one year ago, the actual work of the U. S. C. E. covers but a little over six months. During that time every possible effort has been put forth to gather up the reins which were fast extending, and in trying as best we might, to keep some watch and control over the fast and wide spreading work. The results we place before you to-day must be received and examined with this understanding. Our report must be *general* in character. The time has passed when your secretary can give in the few minutes allotted to him any comprehensive idea of the individual societies. We can only touch on the most noticeable features of the work. Those of you who were present at Old Orchard last year will remember the surprise and joy with which we received the news that the number of societies had reached from 150 to 250. To-day we have the pleasure of placing before you the welcome news that during the past year the number of societies on our list has doubled, aye and trebled, till we now find on the books the record, more or less complete, of 850 societies. Do we need any further proof that God is blessing the work. Surely His hand must be with it. In the whole history of religious movements for many years past, what is there to compare with it? In *five* years it has grown from *one* single society down in the state of Maine to 850 societies located throughout the length and breadth of our broad land, from Maine to Texas, and from Florida to Washington Territory. Starting from the northeastern corner of our land and following along our boundary line from east to west, and in every state and territory, with one exception, will you find societies of Christian Endeavor Along both eastern and western seaboard the work has extended leaving but few quarters untouched. There are societies in thirty-three different states and territories of our land. Of course the largest per cent. in any one portion of the country is in New England, the home of the work. In New England alone there are 430 societies. The reason for this larger proportion is plain. Here the work originated ; here the press and the pulpit have taken it up and brought it before our people ; here are the homes of those gentlemen who were instrumental in the start. Rev. F. E. Clark, its father. Father Endeavor Clark as he has been called. Here also are Messrs. Van Patten and Pennell who have given so much of time and money, and Messrs. Hill, Dickinson and Adriance who have always had the cause at heart. And yet New England has no monopoly of the work. It is spreading throughout the Middle Atlantic and Western States with great rapidity. One difficulty is to keep track of it. I wrote some time since to a gentleman in one of our great western states and asked him if he knew of other societies near him ; the records showed but about eight or ten. Back came his answer, " yes, fifty I should think." The East must look out for her laurels. Why did we come to Saratoga this year for our conference? because we had to. Our western societies demanded it. It was central for the work but whether it will remain so is a question. Thus far I have spoken of the work only as applied to our own country. It is not thus confined. Societies were early formed in the British Provinces. The same rapid progress has not in the past been made in that region that has marked the growth of the work in our own land, still within the past ten months we have been in receipt of numerous letters from pastors and laymen in the Canadas, which show that a new interest is being aroused. One pastor wrote a few days since, saying that what was good for young Americans must be as good for his own young people and asking particularly as to its methods.

In foreign lands the work has won for itself a place and recognition. From the society at Honolulu, in the Sandwich Islands, the pastor writes: "We have forty-one active and eleven associate members. At its last meeting the sciety voted to apply to the United States national organization for admission and representation and authorized me to open correspondence with this end in view. Will you, therefore, be so kind as to present the application of the Fort Street church Y. P. S. C. E. for membership in the national organization?" Evidently they understand the work in the Sandwich Islands.

Foo Chow, China, comes to the front with its claim for recognition in a letter recently received from a missionary in that field. After telling of the difficulties which had to be overcome before the society could be started, she says, " Gradually, week by week, the members gained confidence in speaking and praying, and we marked a decided advance in the interest of the meetings. We then felt it safe to appoint a few committees, and a few weeks since we held our first semi-annual business meeting, and listened to the reports from the different committees. I think we can truly say that the members of each have been conscientious and faithful in the discharge of their duties. Our society at present includes a president, vice president, secretary, and *five* committees To these we hope to add others as soon as shall seem wise, and we hope to bring up many practical subjects for discussion, as fast as our young people are prepared for them. But we must necessarily advance slowly at first. We have just ground for the greatest hopefulness."

In India also the work has found a resting place. A lady in Ceylon writes us: "One feature of the year has been the establishing of three Christian Endeavor Societies whose membership together number 171. Regular weekly meetings are held and the young boys and girls seem to be taking hold of the work in a most encouraging way. The idea seems to be one one which may be well applied to this country, and we hope ere long to show many such societies started in Ceylon and India.

I have spoken of the extent of the work numerically. Let us look at results: In reckoning the following figures we have used only *full reports*. About 550 societies have sent us full reports; such and *such only* have we used in making our estimates that all might be relied npon. The 550 societies report 23,000 active members, 7,000 associate members, making a total membership list of about 30,000, From this number there have gone into our churches direct from our ranks 2,067 young people in the past year. If we may use these figures as a fair average and certainly the numbers will warrant it, our 850 societies will represent nearly 50,000 young people and would swell the recruits for our churches to far over 3,000. What better showing can you ask for? What other instrumentality has been or can be used which will reach our young people to such an extent? Surely it has won for itself an honorable position in the rank of evangelizing the world. The work as you know is not denominational. There are represented eight denominations—Congregational, Presbyterian, Baptist, Methodist, Lutheran, Reformed, Episcopal and Union, while in addition there are many societies unconnected with *any* church, but established in schools and educational institutions of various kinds. The ratio is about as follows: Congregational 432, Presbyterian 110, Babtist 79, Methodist 34, Lutheran 4, Reformed 16, Episcopal 1, Union 20, Undenominational 6, Unknown 142.

Year by year as this work goes on it takes upon itself more methodical and orderly plans of conducting its work. In fine, it is this very fact that it does, *through its system*, appeal to our business-like times and people, that wins for us success. During the past year State conventions have been held in Conneticut, and in Maine; while in Massachusetts, New York and Vermont, conventions have been holden covering in each case part of the state represented. District and local anniversaries have been quite the order of the day, and scarce a week has passed since January 1st that has not recorded at least two such occasions. I shall not attempt to deal with the work done on these occasions, as you will hear that matter fully discussed during the convention.

One new feature during the year has been the formation, in various cities, of union committees made up of the officers and committees of the individual societies in the vicinity. Such unions have met at stated intervals for discussion as to ways and means, and the reports from Lowell and New Haven, where the plan has been longest in use, show decided good gained from this source.

In a few instances the committee work has been somewhat extended. The temperance committee has become more prominent and in many western societies is doing a great work. An educational committee has been adopted in a few instances, thus combining with our work the features characteristic of the Literary Society. A *newspaper* committee is another addition, the duties of its members are to see that all who can not afford to supply themselves with good religious reading matter are furnished with such by the committee. The Honorary and Affiliated membership list has come more decidedly to the front during the past months. This subject will also be treated in a paper by itself and hence needs no words of mine.

I have attempted to give a brief review of the work for the past eight months. I would like to make one or two requests for the future. First of all, send in your reports when asked for. The work has been in many cases much delayed and hampered by a failure to report. Do not in answer to our question as to your knowledge of other societies say, " Yes, I know several," and stop there. Do not inform your secretary that " there are a dozen new societies in your vicinity " and leave him to find them out, but aid us in all you can and thus help advance the cause. During the coming year it is hoped to do much better work than in the past. The society is now fairly started and much time which in the past had to be devoted to the gathering up of scattered odds and ends may now be devoted to aggressive work. It is hoped to place in each state or district some person who will interest himself in furthering the societies' interest in that vicinity. New and comprehensive literature detailing the distinguishing features of the work and giving the papers that have been written thus far and that are deemed of value in the work, will be issued in the fall and every effort will be put forth to hold the ground already gained and to push to its utmost extent the cause we love.   To quote from our trustees :   " The society is ready to respond to all calls for assistance in extending the work among the churches and will co-operate in every way possible in the formation of new societies and extending and strengthening those already established."   Standing thus as we do at this turning point in our year, looking back at the past with the record we have just reviewed, shall we not take fresh courage from our work and looking to God for help press forward in the cause of Christian Endeavor.

ALABAMA.

City or Town.	Church.	Active Mem.	Asso. Mem.	United with Ch.	Permanent Corresponding Secretary.
Florence	M. E.	42	25	22	Rev. L. T. Harris

ARIZONA.

City or Town.	Church.	Active Mem.	Asso. Mem.	United with Ch.	Permanent Corresponding Secretary.
Prescott	First Congregational	9	10	0	Miss May Bean
Tucson	Congregational	32	4	6	Miss Minnie E. Meeker, Ott St.

CALIFORNIA.

City or Town.	Church.	Active Mem.	Asso. Mem.	United with Ch.	Permanent Corresponding Secretary.
Berkley	First Congregational	40			Rev. C. A. Savage
East Oakland	First Presby	43	5	1	Chas. E. Cornell, 13th Ave.
Los Angeles	Congregational	37	21		Miss Adelle Nichols, 804 South Fort St
Los Angeles	Main Street M. E.	17	7	1	V. J. Jacques, 55 Baker's Block
Los Angeles	Third Presby				
Oakland	First Congregational				Miss Alice E. Munroe
Oakland	Plymouth Ave. Cong'l	30		4	Miss Harriet W. Mooar, 444 Edwards St.
Sacramento	Congregational	43			Miss F. De Laguna, High School
San Francisco	First Congregational	50	60		Miss Clara L. Duncan, 626 Park St.

COLORADO.

City or Town.	Church.	Active Mem.	Asso. Mem.	United with Ch.	Permanent Corresponding Secretary.
Boulder City	First Presby	30		2	Miss May F. Walker
Denver	Second Congregational	37		5	Miss Eva Miller, 698 Curtis St
Georgetown	First Presby	36	28	4	W B. W. Gallway, Box 358

CONNECTICUT.

City or Town.	Church.	Active Mem.	Asso. Mem.	United with Ch.	Permanent Corresponding Secretary.
Ansonia	Congregational	44	14	14	Hattie A. Roys
Berlin	Congregational	25	10	3	Clinton H. Bird
Bethlehem	M. E.				
Birmingham	Congregational	23	25		J. A. Coe, Jr.
Birmingham	South Congregational	72	11		Wm. E. Hathaway, 123 Norman St.
Bridgeport	Baptist				
Bristol	Congregational	16	10	1	Mrs. J. C. Cromer
Broad Brook	Union				
Brooklyn	Congregational				Rev. T. D. Barclay
Centrebrook	Union	20	5		Ernest C Spurr
Chapinville	Congregational	37	3	3	Lena E. Kelsey
Clinton	Congregational	52			Fannie M. Osborne
Danbury	First Congregational	34	38		W. S. Brown
Derby	Congregational	20	3		Sam'l A. Eddy
N. Canaan	Congregational	139	7		S. C. Russell, East Haven, New Haven Co.
East Haven	Easton Baptist				
Easton	So. Congregational	35	6		Lettie P. Strong, Hockanum, box 24
East Hartford	Congregational	13	13	3	Miss Martha C. Meeker
Greenfield Hill	Windsor Ave. Congre'l	71		7	F. M. Dawson, 122 Clark St.
Hartford	Congregational	40	12	18	Miss Estella E. Clark
Higganum	Congregational	24	1		Jessie B. Judson
Huntington	Congregational	22	13		Henry C. Cowles
Kensington	Congregational	43	21		H. E. Palmer, M. D.
Litchfield	Congregational				

CONNECTICUT—Continued.

Place	Church				Name
Manchester	Congregational	68	15		Lucy A. Hale, So. Manchester
Meriden	First Congregational	62	1	1	Lillian B Smith, Lock box 783
Meriden	Centre Congregational				Hattie L. Devereux, 233 Colony St.
Meriden	Broad St. Baptist	34	5		Miss Nettie A. Ives, 391 Broad St.
Middlefield	Union	20	3		Herbert L. Mills
Middletown	South Ch. Congrega'l	28	52	5	Stephen A. Billings
Monroe	Congregational	25	14	3	Miss Hattie L. Curtiss
Morris	Congregational	34	10		Flora M. Randall
Naugatuck	Congregational	80			
New Canaan	M. E.	54	48	22	Miss M. S. Raymond
New Haven	Second Fair Haven C.	69	46	2	John E. C. Lancraft, So. Quinnepiac St.
New Haven	First Fair Haven C.	105	25		Miss M. E. Grout, 43 Houston St.
New Haven	Humphrey St. C.	80	28		A. H. Hayes, 54 Edwards St.
New Haven	Howard Ave. C.	77	24	2	Eli Manchester, Jr., P. O box 1199
New Haven	Dwight Place C.	60	2		I. Y. McDermott, 1346 Chapel St.
New Haven	College St. C.				H. C. Booth, box 201
New Haven	Cedar Hill C.	23	1		
New Haven	Taylor church C.	44	4		Miss Madge G. Hamilton, 74 Ivy St.
New Haven	United Congregational	40			Edward B. Murray, box 722
New Haven	Ferry St.	32	18		Mary Atwater, box 207
Newington	Congregational	100			George E Churchill
New Milford	Congregational	35	8		M. S. Giddings
North Branford	Congregational	36	6		E. H. Rose
North Haven	Congregational	20	3		Edward L. Linsley 153 Church St.
North Canaan		70	35	9	Samuel A. Eddy
North Manchester	Second Congregational	66	1	1	Miss Mary Williams, Buckland
Norwichtown	First Congregational				Miss Helen Lathrop

CONNECTICUT—*Continued.*

City or Town.	Church.	Active Mem.	Asso. Mem.	United with Ch.	Permanent Corresponding Secretary.
Plainfield	Congregational	23	18	11	Miss Genevieve Hutchins
Plainville	Congregational	57	6	7	Helen M. Pierce, Whiting St.
Plantsville	Congregational	38	10	3	Eugene Wilcox
Prospect	Congregational	53	19	1	Mrs. W. H. Phipps, Prospect, New Haven Co.
Salem	Congregational	20	5		S. C. Miner
Southington	Congregational	42	34	11	Mrs. F. P. Dunham
Southington	First Baptist				
So. Windsor	Congregational	15	23		G. A. Collins, Wapping
Stratford	Congregational	37	30		H. C. Evans
Thompsonville	First Presbyterian	30	11		Lizzie A. Bennett, Windsor St.
Wallingford	Congregational	28	50	8	F. E. Olmstead, box 481
Wapping	Congregational				
Waterbury	First Congregational	20			Miss C. E. Peck, West Side Hill
Waterbury	Second church				
West Cornwall	Congregational	25	5		Jennie Cochrane
West Haven	Congregational	98	4	10	Frederick W. Mar, box 108
West Haven	Wesleyan (M. E.)	63	11		Albert C. Coe
Westport	Congregational				
W. Winsted	Second Congregationl	54	21		E. W. Jones, 385 Lake St.
W. Winsted	M. E.				
Windsor	First Congregational	26	22	5	Alice E. Morgan
Winsted	First Congregational	41	40	29	Jas. L. Bingham, 47 Main St.
Wolcott	Second church				
Woodbridge	Congregational	14	4		Leroy C. Beecher, box 53
Woodbury	First Congregational	25	1	6	Laura E. Bull

DAKOTA.

Place	Church				Name
Grand Forks	Presbyterian	12		8	Rev. H. G. Mendenhall
Woonsocket	Presbyterian				Mrs. Geo. H. Baker

DISTRICT OF COLUMBIA.

Place	Church				Name
Washington	Lincoln Memor'l Cong.	10	50	30	Janie Tavern, Lincoln Memorial

FLORIDA.

Place	Church				Name
Jacksonville	Congregational				

ILLINOIS.

Place	Church				Name
Albion	First Presbyterian	36	11	4	Fred B. Eames
Aledo	New England C.	61			Elsie Hatch, 69 South View St.
Aurora	First Congregational				D. J. Pike
Aurora	First Congregational	26	13		Abbie Winden, 5th St.
Beardston	Presbyterian	14	9		John McQuilkin
Belleville	Presbyterian	101	112	15	Chas. B. Holdrege, 406 E. North St.
Bloomington	Union	23	6		James G. Curtis
Blue Island	Congregational				Emma R. Ross
Browns	Congregational	47	11	12	E. J. Steinbeck
Bunker Hill	Congregational	54			
Champaign					

ILLINOIS.—Continued.

City or Town.	Church.	Active Mem.	Asso. Mem.	United with Ch.	Permanent Corresponding Secretary.
Chebause	Congregational	35			Emma Schrader, Box 33
Chebause	M. E.				
Chicago	First Congregational				
Dover					
Englewood	First Congregational	30			Miss Emma Hosford
Fairfield	Presbyterian				C. M. Lyman, 52 Wabash Ave., Chicago
Freeport	First Presbyterian	63	21	15	Rev. J. S. Davis
Galva	Congregational	41	5	6	Mabel L. Sandy
Geneseo	First Congregational	50	3	3	Eva Ray Dickinson
Geneseo	First M. E.				Rev Alb Bushnell
Irving Park	Dr. Af'd	30			Rev. Wm. H. Phraner
Jacksonville	First Congregational	35	6		Laura Brown, 110 College St.
Jacksonville	Westminster Presby.	32			Rev. S. M. Morton
Kankakee	B.				
Keithsburg		28			Miss Abbie Van Denburgh
Lake View	Evanston Ave. C.				Rev. W. A. Bartlett
Mattoon	Cumb. Presbyterian	11	23		Rev. E M. Jonnson
Morris	Presbyterian	31	3		Miss Viola Zimmerman
Newman	Cumb. Presbyterian			1	Grace Berkly
Normal	Congregational				
Oregon	First Presbyterian	33	22	3	Clara A. Leslie
Oregon	Lutheran Society				
Peoria					Rev. E. Frank House
Pheonix	Presbyterian	18	1	11	Miss Lulu Coolley

ILLINOIS.—Continued.

Rockford	Congregational	52	11		Ruth T. Mead, 601 North Ind. St.
Washing'n Heights	Bethany Union	31	40	8	Alice S. Barnard
Washing'n Heights	Lutheran	30	3		
Woodstock	Congregational	17	5		Libbie E. Barrows, 2 Clay St.

INDIANA.

Evansville	Cumb. Presbyterian	65	8	10	Rev. W. J. Dacey
Franklin					Rev. C. S. Scott
Mishawaka	Presbyterian	32	5	2	C. A. Loring
Rising Sun	Presbyterian				Rev. H. F. Olmstead
South Bend	Presbyterian	40	8		J. H. Beans, 721 Day St.

IOWA.

Algona	Congregational	39	20		Rev. W. H. Burnard
Ames					Rev. E. C. Moulton
Cass	Congregational				
Cedar Falls	Congregational	27	23	3	Miss Helen Hull, Lock box 142
Cedar Rapids	First Congregational	31	10	8	
Charles City	Congregational				
Cincinnati	Congregational	27	10		Warren Aukeny
Corning	Calvary So. of C.E. (P.)	24	6	1	De Witt C. Hurley, Walker St.
Des Moines	Baptist				
Des Moines	Congregational	23	29	3	Rev. Lyman W. Winslow
Earlville					

IOWA—*Continued.*

City or Town.	Church.	Active Mem.	Asso. Mem.	United with Ch.	Permanent Corresponding Secretary.
Gilman	Congregational	11	33	3	Mrs. G. M. D. Slocum
Gilman	C. Junior Society	12	34	3	Chas. F. Rogers
Grundy Centre	Presbyterian	30	8	10	Mrs. G. M. D. Slocum
Granger					
Independence					
Janesville	Presbyterian				Rev. C. M. Howe
Lewis	Congregational	25	6	2	Laura Norma Gifford
Lynnville					
Manchester	Congregational	40	10		Mary Satterlee
Marble Rock					
Marion	Congregational	40	20	0	T. J. Davis
Marshalltton					
Mason City	First Congregational	35	41	14	Mrs. Geo. Knowlton
Mason City	M. E				
Mason City	Baptist				
Middletown	Presbyterian	11	2	3	Rev. Edwin C. Haskell
Monticello	Congregational	31	41	1	Chas. Clyde Hunt
Newton	First Congregational	45	42	7	E. C. Hough
Pattersonville	Union	30	29	13	
Quasqueton	Congregational	20			Rev. J H. Owis
Rockford	Congregational	27	94	27	W L Patton
Tabor	Congregational	50	21	22	Mary M. McCormick
Traer					
Van Cleve					

IOWA.—*Continued.*

Place	Church			Name
Waterloo	Congregational			
Webster City	Congregational		26	
Winthrop	Congregational	24	6	Rosa Pierce

KANSAS.

Place	Church			Name
Anthony				Rev. J. C. Halliday
Bloomington				
El Dorado			4	
Emporia	Union	6	0	Albert E. Ayers
Geneva	First Congregational	19	5	Miss Della Marsh
Lawrence	Pilgrim	35	15	F. H. Leonard
N. Lawrence				
Paola	Congregational	19		C. W. Trickett
Peabody				
Riverton				
Seneca	Congregational	30	26	Dr. S. E. Johnston
Topeka				

KENTUCKY.

Place	Church			Name
Louisville	Congregational			Rev. S. S. Waltz

MAINE.

Place	Church			Name
Acton	Congregational			
Auburn	Court St. F. B.			
Auburn	Sixth St. Cong.	24	35	B. L. Pitman, 50 Cook St.

MAINE.—*Continued.*

City or Town.	Church.	Active Mem.	Asso. Mem.	United with Ch.	Permanent Corresponding Secretary.
Auburn	High St. Cong.	39	6	17	C. C. Low
Bath	Congregational	34	5	5	Cora Dodge
Bluehill	Cong. and Bapt	28	21		W. H. Gardner
Bucksport	Elm St. C.				
Buxton	Un.				
Cornish	Hillside Cong.	31	0	2	John B Pike
Cumberland Centre	Congregational	48	5	15	Carrie F. Wilson
Cumberland Mills	Warren Congregational	92	45	4	Warren L. Hunt
Deer Isle	First Congregational	19			Jas. L. Haskell
East Machias					
Ellsworth Falls	Congregational	40		6	Albert J. Lord
Falmouth					
Farmington	Un.	41	5	3	Carrie W. Titcomb
Freeport	First Congregational	34	11	6	B. M. Dennison
Fryeburg	Congregational				
Gilead					
Gray	Un.	36	10	1	Annie L. Bean
Harrington					
Holden	Congregational	18	10		Mary S. Wiswell
Kennebunk	Union Congregational	26	11		Eva A. Hall, 45 Main St
Lisbon Falls	Baptist	14	6		W. D. Plummer
Machias	Center St. Cong.	33	10		Miss M. O. Longfellow
Milford					
N. Bridgton	Un. Academy	31	12		M. Abb:e Mead

MAINE.—Continued.

Town	Church				Name
N. Yarmouth	Second Congregational				
Norway	Un.	32	5	6	Miss Addie Buswell
Oakland	First Baptist	30		1	Jeannette Benjamin, Box 205
Paris Hill					
Portland	Williston Cong.	149	34	2	M. Alice Metcalf, 191 Pine St
Portland	West Congregational	51	4		C. F. Bolton, 2 Wharf St
Portland	Second Parish Cong.	66	16	7	Miss H. M. Leach, 178 Newbury St
Portland	Free St. Baptist	41	14	6	Lucy A. Noyes, 36 Winter St
Portland	St. Lawrence St Cong.	60	30	11	Alex Menish, 20 St. Lawrence St
Portland	Plymouth Free Baptist	79	18	8	O P. Wish, "Argus Office"
Portland	First Baptist	79	21		Albert B. Hall, 167 Court St
Portland	Pine St. M. E.	50	21	6	Miss Louie B. Morris, 709 Congress St
Portland	Congress St M. E.	44	12	8	A. W. Puddington, 421 Congress St
Sebec					
South Freeport	Congregational	29	10	5	M. A. Plummer
South Paris	Congregationol	27	1	4	Freenie L. Small
West Falmouth	Free Baptist				
Woodfords	Congregational	105	21	5	Howard A. Lincoln, 193 Middle St
Woodfords	Clark Memorial M.				
Yarmouth	First Parish Cong	37	18		A. H. True

MARYLAND.

Town	Church				Name
Baltimore	Light St. Presbyterian	25	9		Luther Martin, 189 Hanover St
Baltimore	First Congregational				Rev. Wm. F. Slocum
Baltimore	Second Presbyterian	107	27	30	Frank Culver, 52 N. Broadway

MASSACHUSETTS.

City or Town.	Church.	Active Mem.	Asso. Mem.	United with Ch.	Permanent Corresponding Secretary.
Acton					
Abbington Centre					
Allston					
Amherst	Congregational				Frank W. Harrington
Amherst	North Congregational	52	26		Ada F. Baker, Box 63
Arlington	South Congregational	14	14		
Ashfield	Congregational	50	17		Gertrude E. Howes
Ashland					
Auburndale	Congregational	77	6	8	W. F. Little
Attleboro Falls	Congregational	10	1		Merrill Aldrich
Ballardvale	Union Congregational	27	15		Miss S. E. Haynes, High St
Benton					
Beverly	Washington St. Cong.	43	18	2	F. G. Lefavour, 95 Cabot St
Bernardston	Congregational				
Boston	Shawmut Cong.	94	4		John Albee, Jr., 122 W. Concord St
Boston	Union Church				
Boston	Congregational				
Boston	Ruggles St. Baptist				Miss S. E. Kittredge, 9 Cong. Pub. House, Boston
Boston, South	Phillips Cong.	188	68	22	Walter L. Colby, 425 Broadway
Boston	Charles'n, Winthrop C.	77	68	4	L. M. Prime, 3 Baldwin St
Boston	" Monument Sq. B.				
Boston	Dorchester 2d Church C.	35	63	5	Winifred V. Blanchard, Harvard St, Dor
Boston	Roxbury, Walnut Ave.C.				
Boston	First Free Baptist	53	1	30	Clara A. Perkins, 48 Rutland St

MASSACHUSETTS.—Continued.

Location	Church				Leader
Boston	Boylston Cong.	20	13	4	Veta Chandler, Boylston Station
Boston	N.E.Conserv'y of Music	40	16		O. E. Mills
Boston	North End Mission Un.	18	18		Miss F. Augusta Burnett,29 Marion St., Charleston.
Boston	First Mariner's Ch.Bapt.	24			Rev. A. A. Smith, 160 Congress St
Boxford	First Congregational	38	9	6	Miss A. L. Cleveland
Bradford	Congregational	55		8	W. Eugene Ellis
Brookline	Harvard Congregational	71	75	2	Alice M. Libby, Prospect Ave., Corey Hill.
Buckland	Shepard Congregational	33	7	8	A C. Hodges
Cambridge	First Congregational C.				
Cambridge	North Ave. Cong.	88	26	9	Edwin F. Fobes, 18 Beech St., No. Cambridge
Cambridge	Prospect St. 1st Evg. C	50	15	1	Irving W. Cotton, 23 Clinton St.
Cambridgeport	Pilg'm B. "Chr'n Work"				
Cambridgeport	North Ave. Baptist				
Cambridgeport	Wood Memorial				
Charlemont	Un.	18	6		Alice N. Warner
Charlestown	First Parish C.	28	2		Florence Hall, 4 Auburn St
Chelsea	Central Congregational	52	6	4	W. C. Belden, 90 Clark Avenue
Chester Depot					
Chicopee Falls	Methodist	12			Florence Fay, East St
Chicopee Falls	Congregational				
Clinton	First Congregational	28	14		Miss Helen E. Day, Prospect St
Cohasset	Second Congregattonal	26	19		W. B. Nichols
Concord	Trinitarian Cong.				
Conway	Congregational				
Danvers	Maple St. Cong.	74	44		Miss Edna M. Legro, 7 Franklin St
Dedham	Allin Congregational	39	19	1	Eliza L Darling, Box 283
Dorchester	Pilgrim Congregational	40	24		Miss F. E. Whipple, Pleasant St

MASSACHUSETTS.—*Continued.*

City or Town.	Church.	Active Mem.	Asso. Mem.	United with Ch.	Permanent Corresponding Secretary.
Duxbury	Congregational	11	16		Sara B. Higgins
East Douglas	Second Congregational	38	34		Anna F. Hunt, Main St
Easthampton	Payson Congregational				
East Medway					
Essex	Congregational	34	30		S. L. Burnham
Everett	Congregational	37	14		N. W Frye, Jr., Chelsea St
Fall River	Central Congregational	76	41	16	Mary A. Baker, 32 Highland Ave
Farmerville					
Fitchburg	Rollstone	110	3		Janet Y. Wright, 20 Linden St
Framingham	Congregational	34	8		Florence C. Shepherd
Franklin	Congregational	55	19	7	Elsie M Smith, Box 106
Franklin	Baptist				
Georgetown	First Ch. Congregational	34	16		Lewis H. Giles
Gloucester	Evang. Congregational	77	20	8	Blanche M. Swett, 11 Hovey St
Grafton	Congregational	19	26		Nellie F. Fay, Grafton, Box 44
Grafton	Baptist	26	20		Miss M. D. Fisher
Granville	Congregational	14	11		E. M. Dickinson
Granville	Baptist				
Greenfield	Congregational	19	17	1	E M. Williams, Wells St
Groton	Union Congregational	25	10	8	Henry J. Fitch
Hadley	First Congregational	46	4		C. B. Menton
Hatfield	South Congregational				
Haverhill	West Congregational	35	2	7	Edna Haseltine
Haverhill	North Congregational	55	38	3	Chas M. Kimball

MASSACHUSETTS.—Continued.

Location	Church				Secretary
Haverhill	Centre Church Cong.	33	22		Flora L. Cluff, 12 Orchard St
Haverhill	Winter St. Baptist	52	21		Alice S. Farrington, 60 Hurd St
Hingham					
Hinsdale	Congregational	39	16		Jennie Converse
Holliston	Congregational	54		25	Rev. Geo. M. Adams
Holyoke	Second Congregational	50	48	22	Hattie M. Webber, 188 Chestnut St
Holyoke	Second Baptist	68			S. S. Rogers
Housatonic	Congregational	40	49	10	Carrie L Giddings
Hubbardston	Congregational	23	19		Alice E. Underwood
Hyde Park	First Congregational	52	19		Miss Mabel H. Emerson, 90 Fairmount Street
Jamaica Plain	Cong. Christ'n Workers				
Jeffersonville					
Lancaster	Congregational	16	17		Rev. Lewis W. Mowry
Lawrence	First Free Baptist	50	30		Dottie A. Ames, Milton Street
Lee	Congregationrl	96	47	12	Rev. L. S. Rowland
Leicester	Congregational	51			Wm. Henry Davis
Lenox	Baptist				
Littleton	Congregational	32		3	Lois E. Pond
Lowell	Fifth St. Baptist	57	37		Belle P. Miller, 36 Seventh Street
Lowell	Pawtucket Cong.	39	10	5	Lilla Ward, Pawtucketville, Lowell
Lowell	High St. Congregational	61	81	21	Mattie S. Whittemore, 55 Chestnut Street
Lowell	Eliot Congregational	78	93	5	Miss L. A. Wallingford, 4 Osgood Street
Lowell	John St. Congregational	53	25	11	Prof. Channing Whittaker, 42 Appleton St.
Lowell	Kirk St Congregational	96	27	20	Miss Maria A. Mack, 2 Mt Washington Street
Lowell	Prim. M. E.	25	2	2	John C. W. Wilmot, 64 Railroad Street
Lowell	Mount Zion				
Lowell	French Protestant Cong.	30	50	15	Miss H. Caron, 410 Merrimac Street
Lowell	First Congregational	88	25	6	Mary Burns, 388 Merrimac Street

MASSACHUSETTS.—Continued.

City or Town.	Church.	Active Mem.	Asso. Mem.	United with Ch.	Permanent Corresponding Secretary.
Lowell	Mt. Vernon Baptist	27	8		Edwin B. Stiles, 15 Merrimack Corporation
Lynn	Central Congregational	75	11	3	A. R. Phillips, 20½ Stephen's Street
Lynn	North Congregational	74	26	8	Ella E. Severance, 1 Brimblecom Street
Lynn	Christian				
Lynn	Chestnut Street Con'gl	45	13	1	Geo. E. Sargent, 5 Parrott Street
Marblehead	Stone Church, Con'gl				
Marblehead	North	57	21	6	Hannah Tutt, Box 330
Marlboro	Congregational				Rev. A. F. Newton,
Marion	Congregational	34	22		Rev. J. L. Litch
Marshfield	Congregational	15			Henry J. Howland
Mattapoisett	Congregational	32	20	2	Cora S. W Bondry
Maynard	Union Congregational	35	27		Geo Hartman
Medfield	Second Congregational	26	35	2	Edith S. Crane, Box 46
Medford	Mystic Congregational	49	37		Mrs F. H C. Woolley, 8 Court Street
Medway	Congregational	11	16	1	Geo. H. Dane
Melrose	Congregational	72	32	7	Anna M Chapin, R'm 64, 1 Somerset St., Boston.
Melrose	Methodist Episcopal	32			Emma J. Anderson
Melrose	Baptist	67	14	6	S. S. Leighton, 42 Central Street, Boston
Melrose Highlands	Congregational				
Methuen	First Congregational	51	3		Mary E. Sargent, 2 Tremont Street,
Middleton	Congregational	24	21		Lillian P. Fletcher
Mittineague					
Millis	Rockville Cong'l				
Montague	First Congregational	26	18	9	Flora E Kendall

MASSACHUSETTS.—*Continued.*

Place	Church				Name and Address
Monterey					
Natick	Congregational	76			H. M. Wilson, Box 433
Needham	Burgess Cong	39	24	2	Frances A. Carpenter, May St.
Newbury	First Church Cong	15	26		Miss L. F. Mullikin, 46 High St., Newburyport
Newburyport	North Congregational	54	31	4	Fred L. Townsend, 19 Boardman St
Newburyport	Prospect St. Cong	57	22	18	Miss Eva J. Smith, Washington St.
Newburyport	Fourth Congregational				
Newburyport	Old South Cong				
Newburyport	First Presbyterian	28	33	5	Miss Abbie P. Noyes, 72 Vine St
Newburyport	Washington St. M. E.				
Newburyport	Baptist Church	6	24	5	Miss Georgie Teel, 7 Federal St
Newton	Congregational	42	53	5	Mrs. C. G. Phillips, Cherry St.
Newton Highlands	N. H. Congregational	48	22	3	Anna S. Thompson
New Bedford	Spruce St. Cong	13	4		Miss M. E Potter, 165 Kempton St
North Amherst	North Congregational				
Northboro	Congregational	31	5	3	A. E. Parmenter
Northbridge	Congregational	29	6	6	Rev. J. H. Childs
Northbridge	Rockdale Cong.				
Northfield					
North Cambridge	North Ave. Baptist	75	13	2	Warren M. Draper, 292 N. A.
North Carver					
Nonantum	Congregational	21			E. A. Richardson, Newtonville, Mass
Norwood	Congregational	34	13		Edson D. Smith, 5 Walpole St
Oldtown					
Orleans	Congregational	9	7		Miss M. E. Hopkins, E. Orleans St.
Peabody	South Congregational	28	2		Annie S. Thorndike, 117 Main St
Peabody	West Congregational	14	5		Frank K. McIntire, West Peabody

MASSACHUSETTS.—Continued.

City or Town.	Church.	Active Mem.	Asso. Mem.	United with Ch.	Permanent Corresponding Secretary.
Peperell	First Baptist	63			Mrs. M. H. Perkins, 18 Francis Ave
Pittsfield	South Congregational				
Pittsfield	Congregational				
Plimpton	Pilgrim	10			Miss Eliza Ripley
Plymouth					
Revere					
Rochester	First Congregational	20	9		Mrs. George B. Haskell
Rockdale					
Rockland	First Congregational	53	4	1	Evelyn A. Reed, Vernon St.
Rockland	Baptist				
Rockport	Congregational	10	10		Edith Gott
Rockville	Congregational	13	5		Mrs. S. F. Bucklin
Rollstone					
Roxbury	Eliot St. Congregational	45	16	1	Miss Laura M. Marston, 84 Zeigler St
Roxbury	Walnut Ave. Cong.	59	36	15	Mary L. Tucker, 13 Rockland Ave
Salem	Crombie St. Cong.	25	7		Miss M. F. Strout, 22 Linden St.
Salem	First Baptist	64	13	7	Rufus B. Gifford, Jr., 11 Dean St
Salem	South Congregational	38	44		Lilla R. Atwood, 136 Federal St.
Salem	Tabernacle Cong.	46	22		James P. Hale, 27 Mt. Vernon St
Salem	Central Baptist	50	1	8	Miss Luna D. Austin, 5 Symonds St
Saundersville					Miss Annie Killen
Saxonville	Congregational	38	13	13	Rev. M. A. Stevens
Saugus	Congregational	23	6	8	Anna F. Newhall
Shelburne	First Congregational	30	23	8	Mrs. Austin L. Peck, 2nd

MASSACHUSETTS — *Continued.*

Place	Church				Secretary
Shelburne Falls	Second Congregational	46		14	Miss C. E. Field
Somerville	Broadway Cong.	28	17	6	Howard Dawson, 9 Albion St
Somerville	Prospect Hill Cong.	50	17	10	Chas. W. Silsbee
Somerville	Winter Hill Cong.				
Somerville	Day St Congregational	90	40		S. A. Collinson, Newbury St
Somerset	First Congregational	26	5		Wm. S. Gray, Box 176
South Braintree	Congregational	15	26		Annie K. Dyer
South Danvers					
South Egremont	Congregational	29	14	2	Miss Lizzie Wilcox
South Framingham	South Congregational	58		6	Anna M. Mason, South St
South Natick	John Eliot Cong.	42	10	12	
South Hadley Falls	Congregational	43	21		Grace Skinner
South Peabody	Congregational	13	8	2	Lena F. Shaw, Lynn St
South Weymouth		41	30	8	J. Field
Springfield	First Church of Christ C.	83	5	9	Chas. W. Williams, 278 Walnut St
Springfield	Hope Congregational	40	12		Miss Lizzie S. Wheeler
Springfield	Olivet Congregational	31			Ida W. Joslyn, 90 Orleans St
Springfield	Trinity M.(Oxford Lea.)	50			C. S. Winchester
Springfield	Race M.(Oxford League)				
Springfield	North Congregational	63	24		R. P. Alden, care 2nd Nat. Bank
Sterling					
Sturgis					
Sunderland	Congregationol	68	12	8	Geo. L. Batchelder
Swampscott	Congregaticnal	28	11	8	Clara M. Colcord, Box 275
Swampscott					
Tewksbury	Orthodox	22	20		Maude Foristall
Upton	First Congregational	58	47		Lizzie M. Eames

MASSACHUSETTS.—*Continued.*

City or Town.	Church.	Active Mem.	Asso. Mem.	United with Ch	Permanent Corresponding Secretary.
Walpole	Congregational	40	29	2	Miss Helen R. Stanley
Warren	Congregational	33	3	2	Maude N. Powers
Watertown	Phillips Congregational	60	10		Theodore B. Robinson, Main St
Wayland	Congregational	22	26	4	Miss Susie M. Ward
Wellesley	Congregational	50	24	5	W. F. Stearns
Westborough					
Westfield	Second Congregational	100	41	1	Kate A. Sprague, South St
Westford	Union Congregational	26			Quincy W. Day
Westhampton					
Westminster	Congregational	12	7		A. G. Hurd, Westminster Depot
West Medway	Second Congregational	15	20	1	Laura A. Pierce, 46 Main St
West Medford	Congregational	38			R. J. Ford
West Newton	Second Congregational				
West Newbury	Congregational	23	45	4	Annie M. Vine, Maple St
West Peabody	Congregational				
West Roxbury	Congregational	30	24	3	Irving O. Mahr, Maple St
West Somerville	Day St Congregational				
West Somerville	Baptist	41	8	6	Addie L. Buss, 74 Morrison St
West Springfield	Park Congregational	30	3		Gracia A. Smith, Box 364, Springfield
West Stockbridge	Congregational	22	18		Lefe G. Barrett
Williamstown	First Congregational	57		2	M. Jessie Cole
Whitinsville	Congregational	66		2	Rev. J. R. Thurston
Winchester					

MASSACHUSETTS.—Continued.

City	Church				Name/Address
Worcester	Union Congregational	43		4	Miss Emma S. Cutting, 32 Newbury St
Worcester	Old South Cong.	40	2	1	Charles D. Nye (Putnam, Davis & Co.)
Worcester	Piedmont Cong.	55			Rev. D. D. Mears
Worcester	Pilgrim Congregational	25	6		Etta H. Wilcox, 14 Kilby St
Worcester	Salem St. Church Cong.	45		3	George H. Stone, 66 Front St
Worcester	Plymouth Cong.	34	1		Minnie H. Taft, 34 Wachusett St
Yarmouth	Congregational	28	9	3	Carrie A. Gorham

MICHIGAN

City	Church				Name/Address
Almont	Presbyterian	28	7		Jennet Ronan
Benton Harbor	Congregational	36	20	6	Miss Maud Eastman
Benton Harbor	Baptist Church	63	17	8	J. R. Barker
Bridgeman					
Cheboygan					
Churches Corners					
Clio	Union Cong.	7	4	2	Lena Griswold
Detroit	First Cong.	91			Rufus N. Crossman, 360 Congress East
Detroit	First Presbyterian				
East Saginaw	First Congregational				
Flint					
Grand Rapids	Presbyterian	33	1		Susie A. Welton, 133 Mt. Vernon St
Grand Rapids	So. Congregational	39	5	3	Rev. Ben. F. Sargent
Hartford					
Hilsdale					
Ishpening	Presbyterian	36	13	5	LeRoy Christian
Jackson	First F. W. B.	30			Lizzie Feather, 222 Merriman St

88

YOUNG PEOPLE'S SOCIETY

MICHIGAN.—*Continued.*

City or Town.	Church.	Active Mem.	Asso. Mem.	United with Ch.	Permanent Corresponding Secretary.
Jackson	Congregational	52	12		Harry Holton, Box 1800
Kalamazoo	Cong.	30			Helen Cowlbeck
Litchfield	Union	70	40	14	Agnes Gilbert
Mattawan					
Memphis					
Muskegon	Cong.	45	6	10	Lulu Rice, 18 Jefferson St
Mt. Vernon					
North Adams					
Owasso					
Ovid	Cong	12		8	Mary Joy
Romeo					
Saline	First Presbyterian	28			Miss Minnie E. Buckman
Saugatuck	Congregational Church	52	24	4	Elias Oleson
So. Haven					
St. Joseph	First Cong.	47		29	Rev. John V. Hickmott
Utica	First Cong.	6	18		W. A. Abernethy

MINNESOTA.

Bethlehem	Presbyterian				
Carmon Falls					
Duluth	Pilgrim Cong.	66	17	5	Miss Helen L Olmstead, 429 W. 5th St
Glyndon	Ind. Union	20	12	4	Rev. C. W. Bird
Hastings	First Presbyterian	60			Ulysses S. Panelcot

MINNESOTA.—Continued.

Place	Society				Name
Litchfield					
Minneapolis	Second Cong.	85		20	Wm. R. Burns
Morris	First Cong.	20		3	Miss Buttman, 2204 Clinton Ave
Onatona	Cong.	28	12		D. F. Wheaton
Rochester				11	Emily L. Truesdell
St. Paul	Plymouth	31	10		Alice Warner, 21 Aurora Ave
Wabasha	Cong.			7	Chas Whitmore

MISSOURI.

Place	Society				Name
Carthage	Cong.	25	16		Elvero Hoag
Kansas City	Clyde Cong.	58	21	16	A. L. Cross, S. W. Cor. 9th and Broadway
Kansas City	Olivette Cong.	30	7	8	Mrs. L. S. Austin, 2223 Vine St
Kansas City	Christian Union				
Kansas City	Clyde Juvenile Society				
Lebanon	Cong.	20		12	Miss Winifred Serl
Pierce City	Cong.	20			Louis L. Allen
Springfield	Cong.	48	23	12	Emma Hardie, N. Springfield
St. Louis	Pilgrim Cong.				Miss Mamie L. Richards, 1337 Garrison Ave
St. Louis	Lafayette Park Pres.	20	25		R. S. Logan, 2744 Geyer Ave
St. Louis	Mt Calvary Eps.	17			Frank H. Haskins, 3010 Geyer Ave
St. Louis	St. Marks Lutheran	19	5		F. W. Towner, 3400 Caroline St
St. Louis	Second Baptist	60			Clarence Obear, 307 N. 7th St
St. Louis	Third Cong.	20	5		Miss Victoria Davenport, 3507 Cass Ave

NEBRASKA.

Place	Society				Name
Clay Centre	Cong.	18	1		Miss Lizzie Moulton
Hastings	Presbyterian				

NEBRASKA.—*Continued.*

City or Town.	Church.	Active Mem.	Asso. Mem.	United with Ch.	Permanent Corresponding Secretary.
Omaha	Cong., St. Mary's Ave.	34	13	17	Miss Nellie Hall, 606 S. 26th St
Red Cloud					
St. Paul	Presbyterian	20	6	7	Rev. Fred Johnson
Weeping Water	Cong.	38	12	2	Geo. Farley
York	First Cong.	30	2	3	Miss Ora L. Seymour

NEW HAMPSHIRE

City or Town.	Church.	Active Mem.	Asso. Mem.	United with Ch.	Permanent Corresponding Secretary.
Franklin	Un.	36	17		Grace G. Woodward, P. O. Box 137
Great Falls	First Cong.	44	8		Robert L. Ham, Box 161
Hanover	Cong.	39	43	10	Mary B. Russell
Hancock					
Keene	Second Cong.	48			H. C. Aldrich
Lancaster	Cong.	18	5	3	G. S. Jones
Lake Village	Baptist	30			C. H. Read, 155 Maine St
Manchester	First Cong.	44	4		Wm. S. Adams
Milford	First Cong.	41	11		Miss Alice Barber
Milford	Baptist	20			Harry J. Hall
Milton	Cong.	21	4	1	Allie M. Ricker, Keene, N. H.
Mt. Vernon	Mt Vernon Cong.	60	8		Geo. A. Campbell
Nashua	First Cong.	72	27		Miss Josie Stevens, Box 270
Nashua	Pilgrim Cong.	55	13		Hattie A Nichols, Box 1604
Newmarket	Cong.				
Newport	Cong.	30	11	13	Edith A. Mooney

NEW HAMPSHIRE—*Continued.*

Place	Church			Name
N. Hampton		27	1	Grace W. Dunham
Portsmouth	North Cong.	29 30	13	Annie E. Fletcher
Rye	Cong.	32 6	7	Fred D. Parsons
Warner	Cong.	15 7	2	Mrs. C. H. Jones, Box 103

NEW JERSEY.

Place	Church			Name
Belleville	Dutch Reformed	31 16	1	Miss Annette Van Rensslaer
Chester	Cong.	14		Miss Lizzie Cramer
Clayton				Miss Delia Hall
Dover	Presbyterian	51	1	Miss Augusta H. Crittendon
Dover	Reformed			
Elizabeth	Third Presbyterian	65 6	1	Geo. S. Leary, 1155 Washington St
Freehold	Reformed	21 4		W. D. Thompson, West Freehold
Hackensack	Second Reformed	73 2	20	Joseph Barta
Hackensack	Presbyterian			
Jamesburg	Presbyterian	55 18	9	F. B. Everett
Jersey City	First Cong.	87 10		Bertha Chamberlain, 284 Pavonia Ave
Marlboro	Reformed			
Newark	First Reformed			
Plainfield	First Baptist	39 15		Miss Fannie Matteson
Plainfield	Cong.	50 27	6	N. L. Mason, 44 E. 6th St
Plainfield	Trinity Reformed	45 22		Fannie E. Mattison, 53 Somerset St
So. Brooklyn	Reformed			Rev. A. D. N. Mason
Springfield	Presbyterian			

NEW YORK.

City or Town.	Church.	Active Mem.	Asso. Mem.	United with Ch.	Permanent Corresponding Secretary.
Amsterdam	Presbyterian				
Adams Centre					
Bay Shore	Cong.	24	11		A. M. Thompson
Boonville	Presbyterian	33	34	4	Mary E. Anderson
Bridgeport	Cong.				
Bridgeport	Baptist	20			Genevieve Bushnell
Brier Hill		18			Luther I. Tilton
Buffalo	Lafayette St. Pres.	87		3	May L. Perry, 134 Richmond Ave
Buffalo	East Presbyterian	55	5		Anna J. Krummel, 224 Van Rensselaer St
Buffalo	Prospect Avenue				
Cape Vincent					
Carrajoharie					
Canton	Presbyterian	23	21	2	Miss Minnie Walker
Cambridge	First Cong.	22	30	16	Harvey Green, No. Park St
Corona	Union	33	32		Wm. Demarest, Sr
Chittenango	First Baptist	24	9		Kittie Bennett
Cortland					
Deanville	Cong.	34	6		Mary E. Lyman
Eaton	Union	22	25		Chas. E. Hamilton
Fairport	F. W. B.	44	20	5	Miss Carrie E. Pintler
Fleming	M. E.	13	13		Wm. E. Mosher
Fort Plain	Reformed				
Franklinville	First Presbyterian	10	9		Mrs. M. J. Waring
Fredonia	First Presbyterian	82	26	22	Annie M. Tremaine

NEW YORK.—*Continued*

Place	Church				Name
Freeport	First Baptist				
Flushing	First Cong.	67	17	18	J. Willard Demorest, 80 Lyndon Ave
Flushing	Reformed	13	7		R. H. Baker
Geneva					
Glenville	Presbyterian				
Glenville	Reformed	22	2		Abner Smith
Holley	First Presbyterian	25	10		Sara J. Cook
Jamestown	Cong.	32	22		Geo. B. Todd, 12 Fulton St
Knoxboro	Presbyterian	37	5	2	E. H. Dickinson
Long Island City	East Ave. Baptist	30	7	5	E. H. Lowell, 161 12th St
Lyons	Presbyterian	25			Anna C. Boardman
Madison	Baptist				
Mahopac Falls	Baptist	21			Emma J Barrett
Middletown	First Presbyterian				
Newark	Presbyterian				
Newburgh	Reformed	40		15	Nora P. How, 147 Chambers St
New Lebanon	Cong.	26	22	6	Walter Harrison
New Haven	Cong.	55		7	Geo. Hale
Newton					
New York	North Presbyterian	11	10		Miss N. Kamp, 342 W. 31st St
New York	Church of the Stran's C	53	9		W. W. Urquhart, Jr., 17 Lafayette Place
New York	4th Avenue Pres.	75			C. F. Cutler, 51 E. 69th St
New York	University Place Pres.				
Norwood	First M. E.	79	43	25	Emma La Fountain
Olean	First Baptist	21	1		Emma Ramsey, 11 Henly St
Oneida	Presbyterian	150	23		Rev. Samuel Jessup
Palmyra	West Presbyterian	75		2	Emma L. Stone

NEW YORK.—*Continued.*

City or Town.	Church.	Active Mem.	Asso. Mem.	United with Ch.	Permanent Corresponding Secretary
Palmyra	Baptist	45	10		Minnie Scofield
Parishville	M. E.	48	12	3	Miss M. Maynard, 82 Alexander St
Penfield	M. E. and Baptist				
Penn Yan	Presbyterian	32	23		C. P. St. John, P. O. Drawer 85
Phoenicia	M. E.	23			A. G. Shepard
Poughkeepsie	Bapt. Church	107	38		E. G. Dean
Potsdam	Presbyterian	61	37	6	Lottie Hitchcock, 82 Alexander St
Rochester	Central Presbyterian	55	124	67	Alice L. Dunn
Rochester	North Presbyterian				
Rochester	Westminster Pres.	36	30	6	H. B. Allen, 12 King St
Rochester	Plymouth				Miss Ada H. Kent
Rochester	First Presbyterian	60	49		Miss Belle Cotchefer, 188 Plymouth Ave
Rochester	Second Baptist	44	6	11	B. B. Chase, 139 North Union St
Rochester	South Baptist				
Schenectady	Reformed	23	4	6	C. A. Rome, Box 1057
Scottsville	Presbyterian	40	10		Miss Louisa McVean
Skaneateles	Presbyterian	29	2		Agnes D. Gibbs
Skaneateles	Baptist				
Smithtown Branch	Un.				
Smyrna	Reformed				Rev. Walter Condict
South Brooklyn	South Presbyterian	30	3		Harlon M. Seeley
Southampton	Presbyterian	13	19		Celia M. Day
Spencer	White Church Cong.	30	18	9	
Spencerport					

NEW YORK.—Continued.

Place	Church				Name
Stanfordville	Union	17	5		Minnie Bowman
Syracuse	Danforth Church Cong.	10	12		Rev. D. F. Harris
Syracuse	First Baptist	81	22	11	Irving S. Colwell, 4 Wolcott & West Vanderbilt Sq
Troy	Presbyterian				
Verbank Vil.					
Verona	First Presbyteian	47	3		R. W. Vincent
Vernon Centre	Presbyterian	15	13		Merritt Smith
Waterville	Presbyterian	75			Belle Benedict
Wareaw	Cong.	35	3	40	Virginia Lawrence
Watkins	Presbyterian	44	15	8	M. B. Hughey
Weedsport	Baptist	34	4	5	Cripsie L Burritt, Box 454
Wolcott	First Presbyterian				
Wolcott	M. E.				

OHIO.

Place	Church				Name
Akron	Cong.	275		25	Dr. H. W. Pierson, Cor. Main and Exchange Sts
Andover					
Ashtabula	First Cong.	41			Clara Smith
Bristolville	Cong.	25	5		Nellie Maltby
Bridgeport					
Brownhelm	Cong.	7	31		Miss Mary E. Perry
Buxton	Cong.	50	100		J. W. Stewart
Chillicothe		100			
Cleveland	Euclid Ave. Cong.	100			Miss M. Louise Woodward, Cornell St
Cleveland	Plymouth Cong.				
Cleveland	First Church, Cong.				
Columbus	Eastwood Church				

OHIO.

City or Town.	Church.	Active Mem.	Asso. Mem.	United with Ch.	Permanent Corresponding Secretary.
Geneva	Cong.				
Kent	Cong.	28	3		Miss Cyrena M. Wolford
Lexington	Cong.	51	23	15	Mary E. Ensign
Madison	Central Cong.	56	4	23	Etta I. Gilkison, 36 West 1st St
Mansfield	Cong.	31	36		Florence Curtis, Fourth St
Marietta	Cong.	29	2		May Robinson
Martin's Ferry	Presbyterian	80	23		J. D. Dannley
Medina	First Cong.	20	8	2	Wm. C. Savage
No. Bloomfield	Cong.	9	9		Amy Hayes, 48 Prospect St
Norwalk	Cong.	74	10	2	Frances C. Wilder
Ravenna	First Cong.	5	4		Mary Johnson
Bridgeville	Cong.	36			Miss Cora Clark
Rootstown	Cong.	34	1	12	E. H. Stiles
Rome	Presbyterian	53	33	5	A. D. Visscher, Box 597
Springfield	First Cong.				
Stubenville	Cong.				
Tallmadge		22	10		Cora A. Thompson
Vermillion	Cong.	40	22	7	W. S. Metcalf
Wellington	Coug.				
Welshfield					
W. Jefferson	M. E.	28	3	10	Miss Etta Boyd
Westville					
Zanesville	First Presbyterian	49	17		Wm. N. Ayers, Underwood St

OREGON.

E. Portland

PENNSYLVANIA.

Place	Church				Contact
Alleghany	Trinity Lutheran				
Athens	Presbyterian	41	68	9	Eva F. Peters, College Hill
Easton	First Presbyterian				
Easton	College Hill				
Erie	Park Presbyterian	42	21	7	Fred Beebe, 236 W. 7th St
Hatboro	First Baptist	25	6	9	H. M. Kaissinger
Hanley	Presbyterian	27	22		G. W. B. Allen
Kingston	Presbyterian	78	26	33	H. Kochler
Kingston	Congregational	25	5		Charlotte Davies, Slocum St
Kingston	Christian Church				
Lehighton	Evangelical Association				
Mauch Chunk	Presbyterian	36	3		Carrie B. Leonard
Middleton					
Montrose	First Presbyterian	30			Fanny L. Read
Nanticoke	First Presbyterian	15	18		Miss Mary E. Oplengur
Nicholson	First Presbyterian				
Philadelphia	Gaston Presbyterian				
Philadelphia	West Spruce St. Presby	51	20		G. A. Benson, 1515 Spruce St
Pittsburgh	Butler St. M. E.	158	19	20	H. N. Cameron, 256 44th St
Pittsburgh	Trinity Church, Cong.				
Pittston					
Pleasant Valley	Presbyterian				
Pottsville	Evangelical Association	55	30		Daniel Reed, Jr., 108 E. Norwegian St

PENNSYLVANIA.—Continued.

City or Town.	Church.	Active Mem.	Asso. Mem.	United with Ch.	Permanent Corresponding Secretary
Plymouth	Plymouth Cong.				
Scranton	Second Presbyterian	15	2		James Watson, 519 Pine St
Scranton	M. E.				
Sharpsburg	Presbyterian	18	3		F. B. Axtell
Troy	Westminster Presby				
West Mill Creek	Presby. Independent				
West Pittston	Covenant Presbyterian				Thomas Nichols
Wilkesbarre					

RHODE ISLAND

City or Town.	Church.	Active Mem.	Asso. Mem.	United with Ch.	Permanent Corresponding Secretary
Ashaway	First S. D. Baptist	36	24	5	Miss Amy L. Babcock
Central Falls	Congregational	23	31		Miss Desda A. Allen
Johnston	First Free Baptist	27			Miss Emma C. Gifford, Olneyville
Hope Valley	Baptist	21	3		Miss Cora D. Nichols
Hopkington	First S. D. Baptist				Rev. Ira L Cottrell
Johnston	Mt. Pleasant Cong.				
Pawtucket	Park Place Cong.	51	2		Frank O. Bishop, 115 Broad St
Providence	Union Congregational	68	12		Albert C. Day, 81 Canal St
Providence	Cranston St. Baptist	52	1		Emma A. Durfee, 45 Brighton St
Providence	Richmond St.				
Providence	Academy Ave	20	20	1	O. E. Randall, 37 Beaufort St
Providence	Broad St. Baptist	21			S Janette Vaughn, 63 Governor St
Providence	Mt. Pleasant Baptist	13	5		Emma Hobson, 10 Kepler St

RHODE ISLAND—Continued

Place	Society				Secretary
Scituate	Christian Union				
Westerly	Pawcatuck S. D. Baptist	38	44	7	N. A. Collins, 18 Mass St
Valley Falls					
Westerly	Pawcatuck Cong.	20	23	7	Mrs. G L. Clark, Grove Ave

TEXAS.

Place	Society				Secretary
Dallas	Congregational			1	H. E. Knox, Auditor's Office T. & P. R. R.

UTAH.

Place	Society				Secretary
Salt Lake	Westminster Presby	13	1		Mrs. H. A. Newell, 438 E. 3d South St
Salt Lake	Mission School	13			Mrs. H. A. Newell, 438 E. 3d South St

VERMONT.

Place	Society				Secretary
Barre	Congregational	12		3	Miss Florence M. Howard, Box 56
Barnet	Congregational	25	6		Miss Carrie W. Morgan
Bethel	First Congregational	43	25		Lucy M. Graham
Brandon	Congregational	35		2	Edwin H. Dutcher
Burlington	Third Congregational	43	25		Lillie H. Cram
Burlington	First Congregational	87	24	8	Miss May W. Lemon, 103 Pearl St
Burlington	Berean Baptist				Rev. C. W. Davis
Burlington	First Baptist				Rev. F. J. Parry
Burlington	Methodist				
Chester	Congregational	19	4		Susie M. White
So. Royalton	Union Den.	19	23		Pearl Belknap

VERMONT.—*Continued.*

City or Town.	Church.	Active Mem.	Asso. Mem.	United with Ch.	Permanent Corresponding Secretary.
South Burlington	Eldridge S. Sch'l, Union	12			Henry Petty
Springfield	Congregational	50	13		Rev. Chas. S. Mills
St. Albans	Congregational	85	21		W. W. Jennison
St. Johnsbury	North Congregational				Dr. C. N. Samson
St. Johnsbury	South Congregational	70		5	Miss H. E. Blodgett
Gaysville	Union Den.	10	3	2	Kate Kimball
Hartford	Congregational	62	39		Louis S. Newton
Jericho	Congregational				E. B. Jordan
Lyndonville	Congregational	69	3	37	Edward E. Bond
Middlebury	Congregational	42	10	20	Mrs. L. S. Dowd
New Haven	Congregational	21	10	2	E. D. Whipple, South Shaftsbury
No. Bennington	First Congregational				
No. Bennington	Baptist				
Peacham	Union	60			Mrs. Alice G. Blanchard
Randolph Centre	Congregational	14	10		Mrs. Chas. A. Perry
Royalton	Congregational	22	10	3	Inez E Culver
Waitsfield	Union	18		15	D. A. Kneeland
Weathersfield Centre					
W. Hartford	Union Den.	18	14		Rev. S. L. Vincent
Vergennes	Congregational	43	15		C. A. Strong

WASHINGTON TERRITORY

City or Town	Church	Active Mem.	Asso. Mem.	United with Ch.	Permanent Corresponding Secretary.
Colfax	Congregational	25	30		Miss Blanch Bellinger
Houghton	First Church of Christ	15	3	5	Miss Amanda C. Nelson

WALHINGTON TERRITORY.—*Continued.*

City	Church				Leader
Seattle	Plymouth Cong.	50	33		Miss Louise Root
Spokane Falls	First Presbyterian	33		1	F. J. Eaken
Tacoma	First Congregational	10	10	1	G. A. Channock

WEST VIRGINIA.

City	Church				Leader
Charlestown					

WISCONSIN.

City	Church				Leader
Antigo	Congregational	26	3		Edith M. Logan
Appleton	First Congregational	57	34		Mary C. Harwood
Baraboo					
Beloit	Second Congregational	67	17		Hattie Colton, Garden Alley
Beloit					
Beloit					
Beloit					
Berlin					
Bloomington					
Boscobel	Congregational	34			Susie Favor
Brandon					
Burlington					
Clinton	Congregational	29	9	1	Chas E. Peet
Clintonville	Congregational	22	10	4	Rev. A. S. Newcomb
Elroy	Congregational				
Fon du Lac					
Fort Atkinson	M. E.				
Green Bay					

WISCONSIN—Continued.

City or Town.	Church.	Active Mem.	Asso. Mem.	United with Ch.	Permanent Corresponding Secretary.
Hudson	Baptist	40			Frankie Clark
Janesville	Congregational	25	25		F. D. Jackson
Janesville	Presbyterian				
La Crosse					
Lake Geneva	Union Den.	24	5		Emery H. Powell
Lancaster					
Madison	First Congregational	80			May F. Carpenter, 54 State St
Magomame					
Menasha					
Milwaukee					
New London					
Prairie du Chene					
Rivers Falls	First Congregational	58	13	3	Emma Sellers
Richmond	M. E.				
Rivers Falls					
Sparta					
Watertown					
Waupin					
Whitewater					

BRITISH PROVINCES.

City or Town.	Church.	Active Mem.	Asso. Mem.	United with Ch.	Permanent Corresponding Secretary.
Montreal	Calvary Congregational	32	1	sev'l	F. E. Dougall, 294 Drummond St.
St. John	St. John Presbyterian	15	6	4	Rev. T. F. Fotheringham, 136 Leicester St.
St John	Germain St. Baptist				

FOREIGN MISSIONS.

Ceylon . . . . . . 3 Societies .
Honolulu Hawaiian I
Foochow, China . . 2 Societies .

Rev. J. A. Curzan . . . .

REPORT OF TREASURER OF THE U. S. C. E.

Wm. Shaw, Treasurer, in account with the United Society of Christian Endeavor.

DR.

To balance from old account, - - -	$42.85
Membership fees, (annual) - - - -	115,00
" " (life) - - - -	20.00
Sale of Publications, - - - - -	20.73
Contributions from societies, - - -	1401.78
" " individuals, - - -	321.50
Concert account, - - - - -	2.40
	1924.26

CR.

By cash paid for printing, - - - -	$691.23
Postage, - - - - - - -	344,08
Rent, - - - - - - - -	64.35
Office expenses and furniture, - - -	127.56
Salary, Rev. S. W. Adriance, - - -	135.00
Salary, Geo. M. Ward, Sec. & Treas., -	300.00
Travelling expenses, - - - -	103.71
Certificates of life members, - - -	55.00
	1820.93
Balance on hand, - - - - -	103.33
	$1924.26

I have examined the above account and find it correctly cast and properly vouched.

ALBERT W. BURNHAM, *Auditor.*

LIABILITIES.

Bills unpaid to Mr. Ward, - - - - -	$400.00
Deficit, - - - - - - - - -	296.67

If the following suggestions meet with your approval I would like to have them referred to the proper committee for consideration. I would suggest that all churches using the envelope system, or what is called the systematic form of benevolence, place as one of the objects on their pledge cards, their Y. P. S. C E.; the amounts pledged to that object to be paid to the Treasurer, to be used in meeting the expenses of their society, in meeting their contribution to the general fund of the United Society, and in any other way the society may direct.

In discussing this matter with several of my oldest and wisest friends, we failed to find any real objection to it. But we found the

following things in its favor: First—It keeps close and vital the relation of the society to the church, the money going, as it would, from
the young people to the church, and then back from the church to the
young people again. Second—It interests the young people in the
general benevolence of the church. Third—It prevents the multipli-
cation of the pledge cards. Fourth—It will educate the young people in systematic giving, which I think you will all admit would be a
most desirable thing. This plan is the more important because *all*
the processes of our societies are educational to the work of the
church, and hence if ideal methods of money raising are fostered
among young people they will manifest themselves later in the church
when in the course of the years the heavier responsibilities of church
·work rest upon *them*. I would also suggest that it is the *privilege* of
every friend here to leave their name, with one dollar accompaning
it, and an application for membership in the United Society of Christian Endeavor, with the Secretary or Treasurer at any time during
this meeting.

WM. SHAW, Treas.

THE PROMOTION OF DEVOTIONAL SPIRIT; EXPEDI-
ENTS, DIVISION BANDS, ETC.

BY WM. SHAW, SOUTH BOSTON, MASS.

In the topic which is before us for discussion, we have one of the
most important questions that this conference has to consider — a
question that touches us in our most vital part. Take out of our
societies the devotional spirit, and you take out their very life. All
that is left is the dead and worthless form, which has not even an excuse for being. Feeling this, as I do most deeply, I wish the committee had selected some one with greater knowledge and a riper
experience to present this paper and open the discussion. But as
they have not, I hope that you, the strong, earnest, spiritual-minded
men, will give us your thought in the discussion that is to follow.
I take it that there is felt to be a *lack* of the devotional spirit in the
lives of young Christians—and older ones, too, perhaps—or we would
not be considering the promotion of this spirit at the present time.

Prof. Austin Phelps, in a little book published in 1860, after re-
viewing the wonderful progress of the church, and contrasting the
warm, earnest, helpful, working spirit of this age with the cold aus-
terities of the cloister and the cowl of former ages, says: '' This is a
salutary growth. But like every large, rapid growth, it involves a
peril peculiar to itself—a peril which we cannot avoid, but which, by
wise forethought, we may encounter with safe courage. That very
obvious peril is, that the vitality of holiness may be exhausted by inward decay, through the want of an *increase* of its devotional spirit,
proportioned to the expansion of its active forces. Individual expe-

rience may become shallow, for the want of meditative habits and much communion with God. Should this be the catastrophe of the tendencies working in modern Christian life, centuries of conflict and corruption must follow, by a law fixed like gravitation. Our religious organizations must begin soon to *settle*, like a building whose frame is eaten through and through with the dry-rot. Activity can never sustain *itself*. Withdraw the vital force which animates and propels it, and it falls like a dead arm. We cannot, then, too keenly feel, each one for himself, that a still and secret life with God must energize all holy duty, as vigor in every fibre of the body must come from the strong, calm, faithful beat of the heart." If these words were needed twenty-five years ago, when they were written, how much more are they needed now. The spirit of our churches (and this includes the Y. P. S. C. E.) is that of earnest, active work. Year by year we are drawing nearer to the heart and life of the common people, and in countless ways are reaching out and endeavoring to supply not only their spiritual wants, but their physical and intellectual as well. The highest meed of praise that is given a church to-day is to call it a "great working church."

Friends, there is a tremendous responsibility resting upon us to do this work and discharge this obligation. Oh! let us not depend upon the winds and tides of human feeling and experience for inspiration and strength, but let us kindle our hearts at the altar of divine love, and impelled by a mighty power within, go on to the performance of every duty, in the name and for the sake of Christ our Lord. I think you will bear me out in saying that of all the organizations in the church for doing the Master's work, there is none that covers a wider field, or is more exacting in its requirements, than the Y. P. S. C. E. This being so, if we would keep our work from degenerating into a lifeless formality, we must have in our hearts a strong, earnest spirit of true devotion and consecration to God. Of all the sad sights in this world, a fretful, peevish Christian is the saddest. And yet, if we recognize the responsibility that rests upon us as Christians, one of three things must happen. Either we shall be unfaithful in our work; or we shall be that same peevish, discontented worker; or we shall—would that all might say, we *will*—keep our hearts in such perfect and intimate communion with Him that it shall be our joy to do His will. We need *not* less interest in, and care for, the material well-being of those about us, but a deeper spiritual experience and more of the devotional spirit in our lives and in our meetings. "God is a spirit, and they that worship Him must worship Him in *spirit* and in truth." As young people, we need to recognize the fact that there are spiritual forces in the universe that are just as real, and infinitely more powerful, than electricity or gravitation, or any of the forces of nature. And if we would realize their power in our lives, we have but to fulfil the conditions, and the result will be sure. And now let us consider for a few moments how we may promote this devotional spirit. And here let me say that we do not consider the devotional spirit as a gift of the intellect, but of the *heart;* therefore if we would promote this spirit, we must cultivate the *heart religion*. What does a child know of devotion to a mother until he has *felt* and *returned* a mother's love? And the closer and more intimate the communion, the stronger and truer will be his devotion to her. And so it is, in a higher sense, with our relation to Christ. We feel His love for us, and our love goes out to Him in return. But the question I would ask is, how do we *realize* Christ's love for us? Is it not most frequently through the expression of that love in the life and character of His disciples, of those who love Him? I think it is. If I am right, then the thing to be done is to bring this mighty power of personal Christian influence to bear upon each other's lives, so that the stronger may help the weaker, and we may all attain to a life of more perfect consecration and truer devotion to our Saviour. How can this be done? I suppose I was asked to prepare this paper that you might know of one way in which the Phillips Church Y. P. S. C. E. are answering this question, and the success we have had. We have a resident active membership of one hundred and seventy-five (175) or more, embracing all the phases and types of young Christian life, from the *always* faithful, earnest members, down to the careless and indifferent ones, who need to be continually reminded of their duty, and pressed on to its performance. In an ordinary prayer-meeting not more than seventy-five (75) can take part, and so we had to face the fact that about one-half our members either could not or would not avail themselves of their prayer-meeting privileges. And, as usual, the unfaithful ones were those who most needed the strength they would receive by witnessing for Christ. How to reach these, and keep up the strong spiritual tone of the meetings, was the problem. Nothing will lower the tone of a prayer-meeting quicker than to have someone get up and scold others for their unfaithfulness. Young Christians don't need scolding so much as they need the inspiration that comes from contact with a hearty, consecrated worker. Our pastor, whose sympathy for the young people leads him to anticipate their needs, called the committees together one evening, and proposed that we divide the Active Members into bands of *twelve* or *less*, each band to be under the leadership of one of the most earnest and faithful members. The bands were to be made up, as nearly as possible, of those of the same age. They were to meet once a month for twenty minutes, or more, if desired, at any time and place most convenient for them. The manner of conducting the meetings was left to the discretion of the leaders. The plan met with the hearty approval of the members of the committees, and at the next business meeting was unanimously adopted by the society. Perhaps I can best describe the workings of the bands by taking you into several of their meetings.

The first one we will visit is that of the boys of ten to twelve years of age. The leader of this band is a lady whose heart is large enough to take in all the members of her band and many more besides. She gathers the boys about her in a little room in our vestry, at seven o'clock of our regular meeting-night, and talks to them, in a simple way, of the duties and privileges of a Christian, and encourages them to tell her their little trials and experiences in trying to serve Christ;

then they kneel down and each one offers a little prayer.

Our next visit will be to the band of little girls, whose leader (a young lady who loves the children) has invited them to her home. She has for her subject the word *Shining,* and after showing them what it means to shine for Jesus, and when she has time, telling them the Bible stories of God's faithful ones, thus sowing the seeds for faithful service in their little hearts, they all kneel down and ask God to help them to shine for Him. And before they go they want to know " If they can't meet again before next month?"

Our next is a band of young ladies who meet in the vestry a half bour before the prayer-meeting, and after greeting each other with a warm grasp of the hand and a pleasant word, they have a little informal prayer-meeting. Many of the young ladies who before felt it to be impossible to speak in the larger meetings have come out from these band meetings and have offered prayer and spoken words that have stirred all our hearts.

The last band we will visit is that of the young men. Sometimes they have just an informal prayer service together, but at this meeting two of the young men are to present this question, " How can we, the young men, make our influence felt on the side of Christ and add to the spiritual power of our prayer-meetings?" I haven't time to tell you what was said, but it was an exceedingly interesting and profitable meeting. Before I close, I would like to mention a few of the ways in which the bands help us in our work.

First. They are a great help to the Lookout Committee, assisting them in a hundred ways in the performance of their duties.

Second. They enable every member to know and take a personal interest in at least twelve other members.

Third. They give the young Christians an older one who is personally interested in them, and who will help them to find Scripture verses, and about whom they can gather in the meetings.

But the great power of the bands is, that through the leaders and the faithful ones we can bring a direct influence to bear upon those who are careless and indifferent, and through them, more than through the general meeting, we get at the spiritual growth and needs of the members. At the close of the consecration meeting the leaders meet with the pastor, and without going into personalities, report progress and plan for better work.

After six months' experience, we feel that we can most heartily recommend tbis feature of our work to all *large* societies that feel they are losing their hold on the individual members. since the formation of these bands our meetings have steadily increased in power. The spirit of true devotion and consecration has been present in a marked degree, and we feel that much of it is due to the inspiration we receive and the influence that is brought to bear upon us in the meetings of our bands.

In conclusion we would say that we have tried plainly end simply to give you our thoughts. If you should say you knew all this before, we can only say—" If ye know these things, blessed are ye if ye do them."

THE RELATION OF THE SOCIETIES.

BY GEORGE M. WARD, GENERAL SECRETARY.

In a speech delivered before the graduating class in Cornell University some years since, a noted Senator of Maine said: There never has been any *one* man who has seemed to save a nation, win a great victory or turn any great crisis We have had great and wise *guides* to point out the way, and skilled and valient commanders to lead us in the path when pointed out; but it is only when the *people as a whole* uniting together, hand in hand, under the same banner, and and with the same battle cry, have swept onward, that victory was accomplished.

I can find no better figure for describing the aims of the United Society of Christian Endeavor, and the relation which it should bear to the local societies. God has raised up for us in Rev. Mr. Clark one who has acted as a great guide in pointing out the path of Christian Endeavor, and who stands ready and willing to lead us along that path as our commander; our aim is the saving of young souls for Christ and his service, and our banner is the gospel standard. We are provided with guide, commander, standard and cause, but our army is scattered. It was to overcome this lack of unity in our ranks that the United Society was incorporated; to bring together all that power which must attend the massing of so great an army as our Christian Endeavor has already become, and after wise and careful study of our field to hurl this combined strength into the many small breaches the local societies have made, and thus to look for victory all along the line. We would unite our scattered forces into one vast army, doing battle in the wisest and best disciplined manner, which the skill of our leaders, who have made a study of both field and resources, shall point out to us.

I am very patriotic in my figures. Our national motto will just express our relation, " E Pluribus Unum," from many one. Our country has for years been the exemplification of the truth and advantage of union, and our desire is to-day to show you with equal certainty that our motto will hold true when applied to the cause of Christian Endeavor.

Like our National Union, each individual part has an interest in and a part to play in carrying on the grand whole. Each part gains in the work done and the advantage gained by the whole; but on the other hand the whole can only be of the greatest use when each part is loyal and doing its duty.

In a degree each State of our Union is independent; it governs itself, makes its own statute laws and pursues its own line of business through those channels which seem wisest and best for *local* reasons. All this is done as freely as if it existed alone.

On the other hand, together with its neighbors, it unites, for wider

influence and usefulness, under one head, one constitution, one flag,
one name, and through one congressional hall brings to all the talents,
the knowledge and skill of the best men of *every* individual locality.

So of our societies in their relation to the incorporated society.
Each local society is in a sense independant, governs itself, makes its
own by-laws, works through committees chosen to suit local demands
and needs, and strives in every way to build up Christ's cause in its
own midst. On the other hand, however, like the United States, it
may *widen* and extend its usefulness by joining the ranks of the United
Society, thereby gaining as in an illustration the advantage of *one constitution, one name, one standard* as well as the enthusiasm and wisdom to be gained from the experience and knowledge of the many
energetic workers in every direction. The relation was designed to
be a mutually helpful one. Each can and must be of great assistance
to the other ere either can reach its highest usefulness.

From the local societies the United Society asks, 1st., for information. Each local society as it pursues its labors, using various means
and methods, and trying one device and another, learns *by experience*
what are the best plans for the work, and in what the greatest success is to be met with. The United Society asks that you will give
to it the benefit of this experience. It will cost you nothing beyond
a small amount of mere clerical labor, and it may be of great use if
put within the reach of some struggling society placed in the same
straights in which you in times past found yourselves, and from
which they have not as yet devised any means of extricating themselves. 2nd. The United Society asks of the various local unions
reports of a growth, both in number and in grace. It is a very small
matter if some one person is responsible, to fill out a short list of
questions, only two or three of which require more than a casual examination of the secretary's book ; and yet during the past year it has
been one of the hardest things your secretary has had to contend with,
to obtain a full report, in fact, any report at all from the various societies. Just here let me offer a suggestion. If each society would
appoint one of its members to act *permanently* as corresponding secretary, it would relieve us of many of the difficulties under which we
have labored in the past. I say permanently for a reason you will
easily recognize. You change your secretary as often as once in the
year. Sometimes we are notified of this change, sometimes we are
left to find it out as best we may. The result is a loss to both parties.
We receive no report from you, and you, in turn, are not notified of
the events of interest on which we would keep you posted during the
year.

On the records of the United Society the name of some one person
should be entered to whom we could send, and from whom we could
look for correspondence. Should we attempt to change that name as
often as you elect a new officer, the work would be constant, and
would require a new set of books each six months. This, of course,
is impracticable, and in the future we shall enter on our lists of regular correspondents only *permanent secretaries*, and only societies so
represented can feel sure of receiving the news and facts to be sent at

regular intervals to the various fields. Thirdly, we ask of the local societies that you will show your interest and good will in our work by rendering to us your assistance in pushing and recording the growth of the work. It is a great necessity for us to keep posted in the growth and extent of the Christian Endeavor movement, yet it is spreading so widely and so rapidly that it is next to impossible to keep track of all the new societies as they spring into being. Could we, however, have the assistance of all the friends of Christian Endeavor in reporting to us the formation of such new societies as they come to their knowledge, it would simplify the problem very much for us, and would greatly benefit the cause at large. Fourthly, and lastly, we ask your support. The Society of Christian Endeavor has pledged itself to missionary work. Most of the local societies embrace a missionary committee and spend a great deal of time and labor along this line. We are glad that such are the facts, and we wish to remind you of the claims the United Society has upon you as a missionary object.

First, charity though it should not *remain* there, *begins* at home, and secondly, the work of the United Society is distinctly a missionary work, and thus it should appeal to you who have profited by the very cause which this organization is trying to further. Your very presence here to-day is on your part a witness to the love you bear to Christian Endeavor, and a testimonial to the profit the society and its methods have been to you. Are you not willing each one of you to do a little toward giving to other young people the blessings you are enjoying? The expense attendant upon the work of the United Society is comparatively small, and if evenly divided among a constituency such as this, might easily be made a mere trifle to each. A contribution of ten cents from each member of our societies would place us beyond all need of further funds, and I would offer this as a suggestion, or, if your committee see fit, as a recommendation, that some means be devised by which the work shall assume a more business-like aspect; in other words, the position which it should possess, and that a tax of ten cents per capita be levied upon each society for furthering the work of the United Society. Like all other societies which have for an object an aim like ours, the United Society of Christian Endeavor has provided in its charter for a membership list. The payment of the sum of one dollar makes one a member for one year, while the payment of twenty dollars makes one a member for life. A number of societies have taken advantage of this last offer to make their pastor or some prominent workers life members of the society.

Thus far I have spoken of but one side of the question, and have put it on the ground of a duty on your part, an opportunity to do good for others. I have been surprised in instances at the ground taken in some of the letters addressed to the secretary on this topic. Such quotations as the following: "We are thoroughly in sympathy with the work; it is doing great and untold good among our young people. We wish that all the young people of our land might adopt the same method. But what are we to gain by joining the United

Society?" Such quotations I say scarcely seem to us as Christian
Endeavor in tone. There is one method by which a most impressive
proof of the necessity of such a society might be exemplified: Give
up the United Society and let the work go by itself for a few months.
Let all these gentlemen, Mr. Clark, Mr. Van Patten and all the rest
confine themselves entirely to their own fields of labor, and what will
be the result? Each month some five or six hundred letters will pile
themselves up at the postoffice, while the writers, who are anxious to
know how they may avail themselves of the cause of Christian Endeavor, will wait in vain for help or assistance. You will look your
papers through in vain for any news of the Christian Endeavor, and
the work at large will come t. a standstill. You who have the advantage of a year's growth, who are surrounded by pastor and friends
thoroughly conversant with the work: *you* I say, may continue on,
but *what of others?* Nor will you meet with the same degree of success. Cut off the work around you, confine yourselves simply to
your own little circle, and how much or how long will you continue
to grow? I hope we do not need to resort to any such severe trial to
prove our claims. I remember an old jingle somewhere which used
to wind up as follows:

> "A coroner's jury may bring out facts,
> But its rather late to know."

We are not going to try any such expedient. We don't wish any
coroner's jury, and don't intend to prove our facts in any such dismal
methods.

The societies do gain much, or may if they will put themselves in
the way of so doing. First of all, let us look at facts. During the
past six months one half of the three or four thousand letters that have
been received have come from members of societies who wished for
assistance along one line or another. Question after question has
been answered, commission after commission performed, assistance
and advice given, facts and statistics furnished, and hour after hour
spent in aiding, in innumerable ways, the many societies requesting
assistance. In preparing for the many anniversaries the first thing
done is to write to the United Society to furnish lists of societies and
also speakers for the occasion. Letter after letter has come, requesting that more news be furnished to the press, and suggesting many
and varied lines of work, many of them helpful in their way, but all
requiring time and labor on the part of some one. This very conference represents hours of labor, and it is neither just nor right that we
should place these burdens on the shoulders of the few gentlemen
who in the past have done us so many and so great kindnesses, and
have used for us so much of their valuable time which they needed
elsewhere.

Another great gain which it is hoped to furnish to the local societies lies in gathering and diffusing the news and the facts, the new
methods and means employed, spreading them out as widely as possible, that all may learn and gain from the experience of others.
Buxton says: "Intercourse is the soul of progress," and in Christian
Endeavor progress is what we are all aiming at. Bulletins have been

and will be published at stated intervals giving the facts and general news as to the growth of the work. Should it be found advisable to adopt that most needed of helps, an organ, news will be furnished regularly in this way, and a helpful and instructive class of literature offered to all our constituents. During the past three months this work has been attempted to as great a degree as was possible under the circumstances. Matters of interest to Christian Endeavor readers have been furnished regularly to two religious newspapers, while at stated intervals news and facts of especial importance have been sent to *all* the religious papers in the land.

I hope that by stating these facts I have made plain to you the aim of the United Society, and in a measure its relation to the many independent branches. We are trying to push the work into every land and every portion of our own country. The growth of the work as shown by the secretary's report shows that something has been done in this direction during the past six months. We wish *everyone* to partake of the blessings, and we wish *all* the societies to have a hand in *bestowing* as well as *receiving* that blessing. To the present date the relation has been in no way a financial one. The individual societies have assumed no obligation. The work must and has been supported, but *obligation* of any kind there has been none. Nor has distinction been made between those who have and those who have not subscribed to the cause.

The aim, as stated a moment ago, is to further the cause of Christian Endeavor, and to accomplish this by so far as possible, giving to all young people the advantages enjoyed by those of us who march under this banner. My topic is simply to prove the advantage and utility of unity, and to us who are Americans that fact has long since become a self-evident truth, needing no demonstration. It is the old story of the bundle of rods that separately run the risk of breaking, but when bound together by the bands of Christian Endeavor, resist all strain.

Our local societies must by themselves occasionally see trying and discouraging times, times when they need the enthusiasm and advice of others like themselves, times when the knowledge that others have struggled, and an acquaintance with means by which others have been rejuvenated would be of vast help and assistance. Times in brief when a union with others would be for them a blessing and a help. I do not wish to practice what has been called "That hideous gift of being able to say nothing at extreme length," and yet I cannot close without one further appeal to your sense of duty. Emerson tells us that teaching the young is like painting on fresco, the plaster is soft and the colors find a resting place in that groundwork, which in its plastic and purer state is ready and eager to absorb the colors applied, and to bring out the design that the master hand intended. If allowed to harden this power no longer lasts, and the fresco or painting can only be over glaze, and hence but superficial.

Let us learn our lesson. It certainly seems as if our great Artist had designed in this Christian Endeavor a painting applicable and beautifying to the hearts of our youth.   That their natures have easily absorbed it, that it has brought out an added lustre, and made them a thing of beauty in God's Temple is a matter of history and fact.   Shall not we, who have experienced the blessings of this work, think long and earnestly ere we allow the hearts of any of our young people to grow old and harden, ere we do all that lies in our power to subject them to this magic process.

WHAT ARE THE SPECIAL AND MOST INTERESTING FEATURES OF YOUR WORK?

BY REV. HOWARD B. GROSE, POUGHKEEPSIE, N. Y.

When, in the absense of the speaker appointed, I was invited to become a substitute, it seemed to me that the choice was signally *malapropos*, since no society could well have fewer special features than that which I represent.   I may mention those which we have. For example, one evening a month is given to me by the young people.   It is called the Pastor's Night, and I get up my own programme for it.   The Society never knows in advance what is coming on that night.   Sometimes I invite a brother minister to give an address; sometimes I give one myself, or a reading, always aiming to make the meeting stimulating, instructive and interesting.   Then we have an Executive Committee, composed of the officers and the chairmen of the other committees.   This committee has a general oversight, and it is of value in bringing all the other committees within easy reach and contact.   Our social committee found its work very useful in increasing acquaintance in the church, by giving a series of sociables at which every one was introduced to every other one. Some of the results were surprising and amusing, as in the case of one lady who cordially greeted as a stranger another lady who had been a sister member in the church for eleven years.   The new system makes that almost impossible.   Then our Relief Committee did a pleasant thing last Thanksgiving in delivering fat turkeys to those members who otherwise would have had to go without them   The thoughtfulness of this was worth far more than the cost, and was as rich a blessing to the committee as to the recipients.

Two other special features which I hope to be able next year to report upon are a Normal class for Bible study, and an Educational class.   In some way Christianity ought to reach and raise the young people, even to such details as grammar; and where so well as through this Society?   Its aim is to develop symmetrical character, the complete and most cultured Christianity.   The Bible study is of paramount importance.   If the church is to be the power that shall meet Christianity's enemies and conquer threatening evils, then the young people must know the Bible better than their elders of this generation.

Passing now to the most interesting features of our work, I will mention but two points: 1. *The life there is in it.* Young people are full of life. Life is power. Life is what has produced such remarkable progress. Life disarms hostility; drives out dissensions. Life kills criticism. An elderly and critical couple, walking along the street in Baltimore, were attracted by the birds in a taxidermist's window. In the center was perched an owl. "Humph! Jane, look there!" said the old man; "who ever saw an owl perched like that, with head on one side, and that wing hunched up? Pretty bird stuffer, to do a job like that. And look at that foot drawn up; as if an owl could ever sit that way. I tell you, a man that pretends to stuff birds ought to know his business better, and not—" Just at this moment the owl opened his right eye and winked! and without a further criticism they passed on. It is easy to criticise a dead thing. People will always criticise a dead preacher preaching a dead sermon. They have nothing else to do. So they will criticise a dead prayer-meeting or society, and have a right to. But it is not easy to criticise life. And I believe this movement has escaped hostile criticism largely because of the abundant life there is in it.

And 2, the most interesting feature of all to me is *that we have such a work at all.* How long the churches have waited for such a work among its young people. How grand a work it is—the development of all the powers of the young in the service of Christ, the building of character in him. It is far-reaching work; hopeful, inspiring; work for eternity, which alone shall disclose its results and rewards. No matter what the special features may be, let us keep sight of the great central work of spiritual development, and gladly give every energy to the leading of souls to Jesus, and building them up through saving faith into his likeness.

METHODS OF LOCAL SOCIETIES FOR RAISING MONEY.

BY REV. GEO. D. GRAFF, ST. LOUIS.

The question may have been asked by a young christian upon joining the Society of Christian Endeavor, why should the young peoples society raise money? In as much as the society is part *of* the church, *in* the church, and working *for* the church, why then should not the church bear all financial burdens of the society? The best answer to this question can be found in the words, "Give, and it shall be given unto you," and also "Honor the Lord with thy substance, and with the first fruits of all thine increase: So shall thy barns be filled with plenty, and thy presses shall burst out with new wine."

The Bible, then, the only authority of the Society of Christian Endeavor expressly states that if we would receive good, do good, if we would be blessed, bless. Though written hundreds of years ago, these words are as true to-day, as they were then : were written as much for our society as for the church.: as much for us as young people as for our parents.

Since, then, it is right to give, what are the objects that we should give to? The numberless tracts and minutes of this society wich have been so freely distributed this last year by our general secretary, have not only resulted in the formation of hundreds of new societies, but have accomplished an individual amount of good which cannot be computed.

Here then is an object. See to it that the United Society is supplied with the means this coming year to prosecute this work still more extensively than in the past. Again the cry of the hour is, "Young men for the ministry." Let it be one work of our societies to help educate young men to this great and glorious calling by wholly or partially paying their tuition at a theological seminary. and in so doing, help spread the news of salvation. I may say in this connection that two of our members are studying for the ministry, one at Oberlin, Ohio, and the other we are aiding at the Chicago Theological College. He is studying to preach in this country to his people, the Swedes, of whom there are a great many in the western states.

These are some of the objects which lie in the path of the Society of Christian Endeavor.

But the question before us now is, "Methods of Local Societies for Raising Money." Perhaps the first answer that would come to our lips, if asked this question individually would be "Take up a collection." This is the method as in practice in most of our churches, and has both its advantages and disadvantages when applied to our societies. Among the latter might be mentioned the fact that many people, and young people especially, seemingly dislike to have the contribution box passed around at every meeting. This might be remedied by having a stated time to take up the collection—say, once a month—when each member expects and comes prepared to have the boxes passed.

The methods of raising money by giving entertainments of different kinds is one much used by our societies. This no doubt is an excellent way, especialy when we have a particular object in view and can interest our would-be patrons in it It is well to bear in mind however, in connection with this, that as "Honesty is the best policy" in business, so it is in christian work. Always give value for value. Don't give a little cheap entertainment worth perhaps ten cents and charge one dollar for it. Let us also be careful of the kind of entertainments provided.

Give a good musicale, literary, excursion, supper, lawn party or something of this kind. Avoid all "Theatrical Entertainments."

Paul says, " If meat make my brother to offend then I will eat no flesh while the world standeth. Should we therefore, by giving this class of entertainments seemingly sanction or create the desire in others to attend theatres and perhaps in their so doing, be the first step in a downward career, then we are not true "Christian Endeavorites," and the cause we profess is injured rather than bettered by us.

The plan of raising money by systematic giving or the "Pledge System" as it is called, is however, seemingly, the most feasible which has yet came under my obsevation. Perhaps this can no better be illustrated than by telling how it is done by at least one of our societies—that of the Pilgrim Church, St. Louis. At the begining of the year, cards are distributed among the members, printed as follows: "I hereby pledge myself to the amount of   cents per week during 188   to the Society of Christian Endeavor."

It is left optional with the members to give or not as they may choose, but the one is rarely found who does not fill out this pledge, and in so doing subscribes only such an amount as he is sure of giving, prefering to go above, rather than below the amount stated. These cards are collected by the treasurer, and the amount pledged thereon, written opposite the member's name in the treasurer's book. By this means a monthly account is kept with each member, and the treasurer can at a glance, tell whether the pledge is paid or not. Small pay envelopes are supplied by the society which are printed as follows:

" Offering of

M————————————

for the

Month of—————————188————

$—————— —————————cents.

Society of Christian Endeavor

of

Pilgrim Church.

The baskets are passed the first meeting of each month, and members simply put in their envelopes containing the amount pledged. In case members are absent from this meeting owing to sickness or any other cause, it is expected that they will hand their envelopes to the treasurer sometime during the month and be credited with the amount, the same as the others. To those who have never figured on this plan of giving, the results I think will be a surprise.

For example, say in a society of sixty members (perhaps about our average membership.)

5 give 25c per week,   ($1.25)
5 " 20c "   "   -   (1.00)
10 " 15c "   "   -   (1.50)
15 " 10c "   "   -   (1.50)
20 "   5c "   "   -   (1.00)
and 5 " nothing,   (———)

This makes a total of $6.25 per week, or a total of $325.00 the annual income of the society from this source alone.

This is more perhaps than can be accomplished in some of our smaller societies, but with a little push and enthusiasm, this and more too can be raised in *many* of our societies. 2000 dollars was raised yesterday. A grand sum; but we need more, and *why* can we not have it? I will propose later what would seem a very easy way by which it may be obtained. Now let us look at the needs of our United Society. Of the $2000 raised yesterday, setting aside the personal gifts, there were represented but about 150 societies out of 850. Now suppose of the remaining 700 societies 20 members from *each* should pledge himself to give 5c per week—*only a nickel a week*—towards the Secretary's fund and what do we see pouring into the treasury? $35,000.00. If these 20 members only give *one single penny a week* we will have $7,000.

There have been five new societies formed in St. Louis within the past 3 months, and when I return I shall endeavor to get them to send *their* share of this *nickle* contribution to the Secretary's fund. I have enjoyed much this convention and shall return to my home with many new ideas which I shall endeavor to put in practice, and I wish as *my* small proportion toward its success I might induce every Society to adopt this pledge system, and at our next conference our Secretary would find he had ample funds to meet his requirements.

The advantages of this method can briefly be stated as follows:

First.—A regular collection at which every one thinks he *must* give something is never taken. Second—No one but the Treasurer knows how much each member pledges, and consequently no one gives for appearance sake. Third—It is giving to and for the Lord only; and not for the pleasure of an evening's entertainment. And these are the principles which should be instilled in the minds of all our members.

When we have learned that all we have is the Lord's, and at least a portion should be given back to him for the advancement of His cause; when we have learned to give from the heart, bountifully, cheerfully and with simplicity, then the Society of Christian Endeavor has reached a higher plane of usefulness. We have then learned that great truth that " Giving is God's way for Getting," and shall most assuredly reap the reward by seeing the "good measure, pressed down, shaken together and running over " which Christ has promised to give us.

CHRIST'S APPRENTICES; OR THE ART OF CHRISTIAN LIVING.

BY REV. J. E. RANKIN, D. D., OF ORANGE, N. J.

Let this be our subject. The philosophy, the science of a trade is one thing; the art of it, the practice, the knack of doing it, quite another. Says Thomas Carlyle, the great Scotchman, who has now got beyond this world of shams and untruths: "How one loves to see the burly figure of him, this thick-skinned, seemingly opaque, perhaps sulky, almost stupid man of practice, pitted against some light, adroit man of theory, all equipped with clear logic, and able anywhere to give you why for wherefore. The adroit man of theory, so light of movement, clear of utterance, with his bow full-bent, and quiver full of arrow-arguments—surely he will strike down the game, transfix everywhere the heart of the matter; triumph everywhere, as he proves that he shall and must do. To your astonishment, it turns out oftenest, No!" You watch a workman at his bench. You readily follow him with your eye, and in your mind; see him handling his tools, and turning off his work; see why he does this and why he does that; if you are intelligent and observing, may come to know the rationale, the reason of his trade, better than he does himself. Now apprenticeship teaches the art of doing what you see done at a glance. Apprenticeship educates the workman's eye and hand, and whole physical structure. It consists in the doing of little things so frequently that they become habitual, a kind of second nature. You observe the workman, but he does not observe himself. What he does he does almost unconsciously; he has done it so often that the act of doing it makes no impression upon him. The first time an apprentice sets a horse shoe, that makes an impression on him. He tells it at home to his brother and his sister; but when he has shod a thousand horses, he shoes horses almost unconsciously. He can shoe horses as easily as he can eat his supper.

There is a great deal of repetition, and weariness, and drudgery in the life of a Christian; so it often seems to him. It is his apprenticeship for eternity. If Jesus is a master shall he not have apprentices, learners of Him? The theory, the philosophy of the Christian life is easy enough to understand. You may be able to describe a Christian as graphically as a maiden aunt can describe the way to bring up children, or an astute layman can tell a man how to preach; or a newly-fledged newspaper editor can depict statesmanship. But to conceive a thing correctly, to depict it forcibly, is one thing, while the knack of doing it is quite another, can be taught only by apprenticeship; only by prolonged and repeated drudgery; only by precep, upon precept, line upon line, here a little and there a little.

And right here is the source of great mistakes and discouragement. A man has experienced religion. This is one of the technicalities of theology. It needs to be defined like all other technicalities. It means that he has found out the truthfulness of the great truths of the Bible. He has discovered the continent of things not seen and eternal. It is just as much a discovery to him, as though it were a new continent rising upon him, as the new world upon Columbus. For the first time in his life it has become the supreme reality that there is a God, and that this God is his Father in Heaven, and that his Father in Heaven has sent His own Son into this world to save him from a life of sinfulness, and a future of shame and everlasting contempt; to redeem him to celestial activity. He has found that this Son of God is son of man; his brother man. He has looked at it; it has seized hold of him so that he never can shake it off, so that he never can be the man he once was; that is, never can live in forgetfulness of it.

His whole being is inarched as by new heavens and a new earth. And he begins at once, to try to please God, to love him with all his heart, and his neighbor as himself, to take upon himself the burdens of a lost world. This is the whole philosophy, the whole science of religion. "We love him because he first loved us." "If ye love me, keep my commandments."

But religion is an art, as well as a science. And this art is not taught by weekly attendance on the sanctuary, or the prayer-meeting. Nothing but apprenticeship will teach it: nothing but the drudgery of doing little things, garble things, so they seem to outsiders, to us in our impatience, over and over again; day after day, year after year. Do you think that a man can vault into that crowning grace of Christian charity; of suffering long and being kind; of thinking no evil, of bearing all things, and believing all things, and hoping all things, as he would vault into a saddle; by some instantaneous change, under the power of God? His old nature has got to be broken to the saddle. He will have the germ of it, the beginning of it, but it will not be the grace in full bloom; it will take years to bring that.

To-day, he has experienced religion. He has found it out for himself, and needs no man to tell him. He has talked with the minister, or the revivalist, or some Christian leader, and they have pronounced him all right, doubtless he is all right. But then, he is only an apprentice; he has just bound himself out to the great Master, to do what He has for him to do; to become what he would have him become. The papers have been signed and sealed; and now he goes to work, to become in temper, in speech, in habit, whether of body or of mind, just what he conceives will be pleasing to God. He acknowledges the duty and undertakes, with the help of God, to perform it. With a kind of awful admiration he looks at the mature Christian; the man or woman that has been serving an apprenticeship for twenty, thirty, forty years, and the art of Christian living seems to him just as easy, as natural, as the theory. That self-control, that patience under provocation, that avoiding of even the appearance of evil; that doing good as one has opportunity, that giving to God, as God has prospered him; that holy living, that whole effect, so easy and graceful, and yet so sensible, it seems to him, in his temporary enthusiasm, that it is just before him; he can attain it at the very beginning. It is just as it is with the apprentice-boy. As soon as he ties on the apron he thinks he is to all intents and purposes, master of the art; but is he? The very first day, perhaps, this young disciple discovers that the power of habit with him, is all contrary to the kind of life which he has begun to live. He is quick-tempered and out-spoken, when anything crosses the grain with him. When he has felt anger, he has always given expression to it, and before he dreams of his danger, he finds himself in a raging heat, and giving utterance to very ill-tempered words. He is shocked at himself. He is bewildered. What is this new religion worth if it does not keep a man from getting mad with his neighbor, or his work, or his lot, if it does not keep him from intemperate speech?

Now, I do not doubt that a great many people have gone backward from this very point. They have said to themselves, " Well, this is not religion, where a man is just as quick-tempered as he was before he experienced it, or where he is just as envious of another, or just as revengeful." The apprentice-boy might as well say : " Well, I am no blacksmith, if I cannot shoe a horse the first trial, as well as my master ; " or, I am no watchmaker, if I can not make a watch the first trial." Well, it is true. They are only apprentices, learners, diciples, and that is all the Christian is. The Christian has put himself under the tuition of Christ, that he may learn the art of Christian living ; not learn it intellectually, for he knows it intellectually already ; not learn it as an aspiration or aim, for thus he has already learned it ; but learn the knack of it, how to practice it. And he can not gain this knowledge without doing it over and over again ; till the new nature has become second nature. How many a man has wished that he could play well on a musical instrument ; a flute, a piano, an organ. And he has gone to some master for instruction. What does that master do? Does he undertake to teach him some of those fine pieces, which have so entranced his soul, so lifted him up above himself and all material things? He begins by teaching him how to hold his elbows, his hands, his fingers ; how to run up and down the scale. If you have ever lived near an institution where pupils were taking their first lessons in music, you will never forget the ceaseless repetition, the endless monotony, the eternal drudgery of the instruction book. Day after day, week after week, month after month, year after year, it is the same thing over and over and over again ; up the scale and down the scale, down the scale and up the scale. But hy and by there comes release ; there comes liberty ; there comes mastery. The key-board becomes almost plastic and the instrument a living. The hands that were stiff and awkward, the fingers that felt their way gropingly, as though they were blind, seem to become instinct with life and soul ; seem to think and feel and throb with emotion. Then there is execution. What taught them this freedom, this grace, this brilliancy? It was that humdrum drudgery ; that fingering and pounding, that line upon line, precept upon precept ; here a little and there a little.

The mistake which many people make with regard to what constitutes a man a Christian, is precisely here. They think that one must be perfect in order to be entitled to the name. They admit that they are trying to lead a Christian life, so far as they can understand it ; that they take the words of the Lord Jesus as their authority ; that they depend upon Him for acceptance with the Father, and look to having likeness to Him, as their title to Heaven. But, they say, " I have made little or no progress as yet. I have attained little mastery over myself, or my easily besetting sins. I durst not profess the name of Christ, lest I bring dishonor upon his cause." But to be a christian is to be a pupil of Christ ; not a pupil upon this form or that form ; not a pupil ready for a diploma ; but simply and solely a pupil, an a-b-c-d-arian, trying to pick out the letters. Does a man need to be able to play like   Thalberg in order to venture to call himself a pupil of Thalberg?

If Christianity is an art as well as a theory; if the head has to be educated to think Christian thoughts and the eye to become a Christian's eye; the ear to become a Christian's ear; the tongue to speak like a Christian; the hands to handle and the feet to walk like a Christian; the heart to beat with Christian pulsations; then one who would be a christian has two things to do.   He has to put off the old man, with his head, and eyes, and ears, and tongue, and hands and feet; and put on the new man, with his new members.   In other words he is to bring himself, in all departments of his being, under the law of love to man and love to God, which the Lord Jesus taught and illustrated when he walked here among men; he has to learn to execute that law of love as the pianist learns the piano.   And the world is the school room, and human life is the term time, in which he is to do this.   If he has been brought up by judicious Christian parents and has yielded to Christian training in his childhood, he may have already formed the habits of a Christian; I mean the outward habits, though perhaps, also, the inward habits of a Christian.   And I believe we are in danger of thinking too lightly of the importance of correct habits.   When we consider how slowly and painfully correct habits are formed, and how mighty they are, it is not a small thing to say that a young man has correct habits.   It is previous incorrect, immoral, sinful habits that prove too strong for Christian resolutions. We have all seen it, again and again, how men whom we believe to be good men, I mean in purpose of heart and aim of life, Christian men; men who have been for years disciples, learners of Christ, are in some hour of weakness overthrown by the power of previous habit, prove as weak as water, not in principle, not in intention, but in of power resistance, because their nature has been so undermined by habits of indulgence.

Of course, I insist upon this, that however Christian a man's outward conduct may be, his habits as apart from his character form his purpose in life.   There is nothing necessarily vital in this, nothing central and decisive in it.   I believe that there may be more of the spirit of Christ, more of determined hostility to the kingdom of evil in a man who, from the previous dominion of evil habits, is sometimes overtaken by a fault, than in many a man whose outward conduct is faultlessly Christian, in a man who sometimes sins with his tongue or from social indulgence, than in many a man who bridles his tongue and never breaks the temperance pledge.   And yet, I think the time is come when Christian people may well set a higher value upon correct outward habits.   It is, indeed, a great thing that the grace of God can help a man of incorrect habits, who has been profane and sensual, who has been an infidel and a blasphemer, who has disabled himself by habit, for almost every good word and work; it is a great thing, I say, that the grace of God can give such a man dominion over himself; power to break and trample beneath his feet the chains of habit, help him to that freedom where with the truth makes free.

And the man is a good deal more to be felicitated on his entrance up on the Christian life, who has never formed such habits, who has never been a bond-slave to overt acts of evil, who has never undermined the foundations of his moral character, who has never trifled with the dictates of his conscience. Because all this has to be undone, all this has to be counteracted; new habits have to be laboriously formed; just as the architecture of the ant-hill is, grain by grain, here a little and there a little. A foot may crush it in a moment. It takes thousands of little laborers to replace it.

The Christian religion, Christian living is an art, as well as a science. And just where men find the most discouragement, they ought to find the most encouragement. They have no right to expect perfection at once, whether in themselves or in other people. One thing they have a right to expect, daily habitual efforts to become perfect; daily exercise unto Godliness.

A young man goes for the first time to the gymnasium. He tries the horizontal bars and goes plump down through them as though he were a lump of lead; the perpendicular bars, and can hardly raise himself from the place where he stands; and so he goes the whole round of gymnastics, only to discover his own incompetency. Six months from now you shall see that fellow, as agile as a squirrel, go flying through the air as though he had wings; with hands hard, muscles developed, and his whole physical structure full of springiness. How has he done it? Has he done it by aspirations merely? By precepts merely? By watching others? He has done it by drudging there day after day, day after day. True, it was often commonplace and a weariness. But he did not falter; he persevered; he exercised himself unto this mastery which he has attained; unto this development of the physical power that lay dormant within him.

Just so, Christian living is a system of gymnastics, to develop men into the fullness of the stature of Christ Jesus. The new birth makes them new creatures in Christ Jesus. They often reach a certain stature and come to a stand-still; because they cease doing they are dwarfed, headed-in, by measuring themselves by themselves, and comparing themselves among themselves. Or they are disheartened at the length of the way; forgetting that every step brings them nearer the end; that every act of right-doing confirms the habit of right-doing; that every sincere prayer confirms the habit of prayer; and that their outward actions of the outer man are all the time working inward upon the proportions of the inner man, just as the chisel of the sculptor works inward to that ideal which to his imagination, nay, to his prophetic will, lies imprisoned in that block of marble; not a stroke, not a measurement in vain.

I know just how people sometimes feel, if they do not express it; this continual round of Bible-reading, prayer-meetings, giving to benevolent objects, attendance upon the sanctuary, this sort of treadmill circuit to keep the wheel of Christianity turning over and over; what does it all amount to? Can you not devise some new doctrines, or new methods, some new gymnastics, that shall give us a little variety?

Ah, the very power that is in acts of obedience, is in the fact that they are done over, and over, and over again, until they become the habit of the soul! until the soul lives and moves and has its being in them. Great givers are made like great rivers, from little fountains. I know the advantage of getting out of the ruts; of trying to find a new name or a new method for an old thing. It jolts a man, and wakes him up. But let us not forget that there is something to be said in favor of ruts. Ruts are only well-worn routes. The French is sweeter than the English. "Train up a child in the way he should go;" the way, the route, the rut! It is difficult to get out of the ruts, and therefore the safety of them. "And when he is old, he will not depart from it." This means, that when he comes to the sense of his own might, his own independence, of what responsibilities are on him, he will hold to the way in which he has been trained up; the ruts in which you started the wheels of his childhood; it takes a jolt to get him out of them. And this brings us back to the fact, ridiculed by the cavilers against God's methods, that the spirit of the Christian is always in its childhood; never grows old, never takes on airs, becomes unteachable. "Whom," says the prophet, "shall he teach knowledge? and whom shall he make to understand doctrine? Them that are weaned from the milk, and drawn from the breasts." It is childhood made permanent here; glorified and made eternal there. This is Christianity; Jesus expressly teaches us that no man can enter the kingdom of God, who does not receive it as a little child. But what happens after he enters? Having secured admission, can he dispense with that childlike spirit? Is it a thing derogatory and unworthy of him? It is an eternal characteristic of his soul!

We have been talking about apprenticeships and schools, but, after all, we cannot do better than to come back to that little child, that Jesus took and set in the midst of the twelve theologians, who were in eager discussion around him. "Now, here is my kingdom in its beginning; in its type. How did this little child learn to speak, learn to walk? Limber as it is in its every limb, feeling its life everywhere; everywhere natural, everywhere itself; a few months since, it scarcely ventured out of its mother's lap; it could not stand without clinging to her, without crowding a chair before it. A few years ago, its mind was wrapped up in pulpy unconsciousness; a few years later in life, and it shall be just as wise as the wisest of you. It shall understand all mysteries and all knowledge. It shall be able to make and unmake institutions. It shall be able to calculate the coming and the going of the heavenly bodies. And the law of its increase, is the law of increase also in the kingdom of God. With it, habit becomes second nature. It is but a bundle of habits. "Such is my kingdom."

Let us be very sure that it is not without the deepest significance that Jesus teaches us about the new birth; about receiving the kingdom of God as a little child: about desiring the sincere milk of the word, that we may grow thereby into the stature of a Christian manhood. This is not mere figurative language. It is more than that. It unfolds the *science*, the *art*, of *true religion*,

Just as your little child looks up into your face, so confidingly, so lovingly, look ye up into the face of your Heavenly Father; just as he tries to be like you, loves to imitate and repeat you; so be ye to your Heavenly Father; holy, because He is holy, perfect, as He is perfect. And remember, that just as childhood is made up of little details of aspiration and struggle; of minute incidents, which only a mother hides in her heart, as indicative of character, real or potential; so there is nothing too minute, too commonplace, in the drudgery of your daily life, in your exercise unto godliness, to be unnoticed by your Heavenly Father; nothing that you feel, or say, or do, that is indifferent to Him. And remember, also, that just as the continual dropping of water wears away the stone; just as the repeated stroke of the pencil builds up the picture, of the chisel shapes the marble; so do you teach yourselves *Christian* habits; do you learn to practise the art of Christian living; precept upon precept, line upon line; here a little, and there a little.

And let no man hesitate about beginning the habits of a Christian, even before he dare call himself by the name. For, just as surely as life in the leaves and branches of a tree reacts upon life in the roots and co-operates with it, so surely do Christian habits react upon the mind and heart of him who expresses himself in them. I like to find men, who do not call themselves Christians, who have family prayers, which so many Christians omit. I like to find men, who do not call themselves Christians, who are generous in alms-giving; who put money into the treasury of the Lord; who love to help religious institutions; who take their fair share of the responsibility of sustaining them. And I think of the words of Jesus: "Forbid him not; for there is no man which shall do a miracle in My name, that can lightly speak evil of Me. For he that is not against us is on our part." Doing Christian acts, forming Christian habits, bearing Christian burdens, learning the art of Christian living; let us be very sure that these things are not matters of indifference to our Heavenly Father, and cannot be lost, in their influence upon character. And let us all remember this, that the difference between a man whose religious exercises are easy and natural, and seem to flow out of the fullness of his soul; in whose lips is the law of kindness; who gives as God has given to him, and whose citizenship is in Heaven; and any other man who has just begun to lead a Christian life, and who has yet to determine his citizenship; is in the fact that while they both know the *science* of Christian living, only the first has exercised himself in the *art;* has submitted to that repetitious drudgery in little things, which has perfected him into the likeness of the Lord Jesus; which has ripened him for glory; and that by that same process we may become like him. Precept upon precept, precept upon precept; line upon line, line upon line; here a little, and there a little. Thus becomes the apprentice like the Master!

O, thou man, skilled in many arts, trained to think, trained to speak, trained to self-mastery for reputation's sake; O woman, with all thy gettings and accomplishments, how is it? Dost thou neglect

that mastery of self which comes from giving all diligence, to add to
your faith, virtue; and to virtue, knowledge; and to knowledge,
temperance; and to temperance, patience; and to patience, Godliness; and to Godliness, brotherly kindness; and to brotherly kindness, charity? Dost thou neglect that patient continuance in well-
doing which makes well-doing thy second nature, the expression of
the new man in Christ Jesus which thou hast become? Thou hast
put thyself to school, to school duties, to home duties, to society
duties, to duties to the public; thou hast gained many a conquest
over other departments of thy nature and of life; what hast thou to
say to this Jesus of Nazareth? This is what He says again to thee:
"Take My yoke upon thee, and learn of Me; for I am meek and
lowly in heart; and thou shalt find rest to thy soul." Wilt thou take
Jesus as thy Master? Wilt thou take this life as an apprenticeship to
Him, as thy Master? Wilt thou learn of Him?

And thou, too, (my brother, my sister) drawing toward that time
when to thee the fashion of this world will pass away; when all
earth's laurels, won and worn, will lie withered upon thy dead brow;
hast thou no aspiration for that self-conquest which will fit thee for
the companionship of those who have washed and made white their
raiment in the blood of the Lamb? Art thou content to pass out
from this training-school of the Master without having ever learned
of Him? Wilt thou take as thy heritage hereafter an eternity of un-
rest, because thou wouldst not here seek Him, who alone can give us
rest?

UNION OF LOCAL SOCIETIES.

BY ELI MANCHESTER, JR., NEW HAVEN, CONN.

Perhaps one of the best ways in which to open this discussion on
the "Union of Local Societies" will be to ask, What are some of the
advantages to be gained from such union? In attempting to answer
this question, then, perhaps I may be allowed the Yankee's privilege
of asking another. If so, I would ask, What are the advantages we
expect to gain from gathering here on this and the other days of the
conference? What are we, may I ask, but a union of local societies?
Will this meeting, then, aid us in our work as we go back to our several fields of labor? Yes! emphatically, Yes! I hear you answer,
and I agree with you most heartily, and say I believe that as we gain
the advantages of encouragement, strength, inspiration, zeal, greater
love for, and interest in, the work, and much else from *these* meetings; so we gain the same, though perhaps in a somewhat less degree, from a union gathering of our local societies from time to time.
While these are *some* of the advantages to be gained, I believe there
are many more, but I will mention and dwell upon only two or three
which seem to me to be most prominent, leaving the others to be

drawn out by the discussion which follows.

The old and well-known adage, " In union there is strength," will apply here very well ; and perhaps this is one of the *greatest* advantages to be gained in union. Our meeting together from time to time, different divisions of one large army, uniting our hearts and voices in prayer and praise, comparing notes regarding our progress, consulting and advising together about the most important of all life's work, the forming of our Christian character, and endeavoring to gain knowledge, that we may be better fitted to approach our friends on the subject of their soul's welfare ; all this, I say, will surely bring us strength, encouragement and inspiration.

In the second place, I believe this union will bridge, or at least aid in bridging over, that gulf which we so often find between the different churches. If we look at this gulf through denominational glasses, it appears much wider than otherwise ; but looking at it as Christians simply, it is then altogether too wide. I believe I speak the minds of the pastors and lay workers gathered here to-day when I say that we find, as we look over our work, that we encounter this gulf far too often. It must be filled up or narrowed so that the members of the different churches, aye! even of the different denominations, can grasp hands and join hearts together in the work of winning souls for Christ. If, then, this Union of Local Societies of Christian Endeavor in the different cities and towns will in any way accomplish or aid in accomplishing this work, I say with all my heart, let us form unions wherever we find two or more societies near each other.

But, you ask, will it aid in this needed reform. I believe it will, if in no other way than by bringing together every month or two months the young people of the churches and getting them acquainted with each other. I have been able to attend the whole of but one of the meetings of our New Haven Union, and have dropped in at the close of only three others, yet in the little time spent, I have met and become acquainted with a good many Christian Endeavor workers whom I had never met before. If, then, this is true of one who only hears the last hymn or perhaps a little more, what must it bring to those who get to the meeting before it opens, and then find time for conversation, and also have the pleasure of meeting the members during the recess which occurs for this especial object.

Yes, I believe the union will promote acquaintanceship and friendly feeling between the young people of the several churches, and thus will be of great value and advantage to us in our work. But this is not all. There are the devotional exercises in which to engage, there are the topics of vital interest and importance to our work to be presented and discussed, there are addresses to listen to ; all of which will instruct and aid us in Christian Endeavor, broaden our views, and thus enlarge our fields of usefulness in the Master's service.

The matter of our discussions claims more than a mere passing notice. If subjects like the work of some of our committees, our prayer-meetings, and how to improve them, our social gatherings, or topics of similar interest with which our members, even the youngest, are more or less familiar, are brought up for discussion at our union meetings. I believe the result will be that many more of our members will be encouraged to speak their minds on these subjects, and thus overcome, to a great extent, that feeling of diffidence which keeps so many of our young people from participating in our public meetings. Do not understand me to advocate precociousness or forwardness on the part of any of our young people, for that I would avoid. But this I do believe, that ere very long, we who are the young people of to-day must take upon ourselves the duties and responsibilities which now rest upon our elders. Hence we should be ready to bear these burdens gracefully, and should be able to clearly express in words what we have in mind regarding any point of debate, whether it be secular or religious in nature.

In short, then, it seems to me that one of the best ways in which we can benefit our local societies and our individual members is by bringing them together, whenever practicable, in conference, convention or union meeting, as the case may be; thus opening the way for mutual acquaintanceship and interchange of ideas and views regarding the work in hand.

The old adage, " If a thing is worth doing at all, it is worth doing well," loses none of its force by reason of age; hence I would say, that in arranging for the union meeting, we should use much care that only such matters are brought up, and such speakers or writers procured, as shall prove not only interesting but instructive, and thus keep the tone of our meetings just as high as possible.

In proportion, then, to the care taken in arranging for and conducting these meetings, depends the advantages we gain. While I am a firm believer in organization and organized work, I am also a firm believer in personal work, and feel that many times personal work is productive of the most good, not only to those upon whom the labor is spent, but also to those who do the work. Hence, if the union gathering, with its methods of work and its opportunities and privileges open to all, will in the least degree aid in prompting and encouraging us to, or preparing us for, personal work, its value to us who are engaged in this branch of the Master's service is quite evident. I believe it *will do*, yes, *has done*, this very thing, and perhaps, then, this is *one* of the *greatest*, if not *the* greatest, advantages to be gained from " local union."

DR. DEEMS' SERMON.

Rev. Dr. Deems preached a very able and interesting discourse, taking for his text Second Kings 6.17:

" And Elisha prayed and the Lord opened the eyes of the young man and he saw."

Attention was first called to the simple and picturesque tableau presented in the text. There were only two men, an old man and a young man. The old man was a power in the kingdom, was well known, was crowned with honors from God, a man whose name will live forever. The young man was unknown, had no position in society, was a mere valet, Elisha's body-servant. In a time of great trial and peril the young man was carried away by his weak fears. All seemed lost. What can we do? he asked his mother. "We;" all depends upon who the "we" are. If all are as weak of faith as this servant, nothing can be done. The troops of the king will capture and the cruelty of the king will destroy them. But when "we" includes an Elisha, that crowd of two has behind it for resources all the battalions commanded by the Lord of hosts. The weak fear of the young servant and the strong faith of the old prophet made a striking contrast and a sublime combination. While one saw the regiments of men and of time, the other beheld the regiments of God and of eternity.

Together, it was shown that there were exhibited the marvelous capabilities which human nature had, of being an organ for the use of the invisible and spiritual powers of the universe, as well as its capability of being modified and enforced in itself by the unseen. The older man was taken as an example of the prophetic gift frequently exhibited in holy Scripture. Here at some length the preacher showed that the prophetic gift was very distinct from clairvoyance and from the highest genius, as well. Whenever men speak of the inspiration of Shakespeare or Goethe as the same as the inspiration of Isaiah or Elisha they speak in ignorance or in carelessness. It is important that the characteristics of the prophetic gift be well understood, and Dr. Deems took some time in setting it forth. One distinctive mark was that in no instance was it merely a physical or merely a psychical faculty, or a combination of both, as clairvoyance or genius have always been. It was not a natural, not a usual gift. In each case it was a special gift of God to the selected individual, and frequently to such as seemed to have neither the bodily nor the spiritual marks of one likely to receive such a gift. Then, again, it was never for general purposes, such as the promotion of high literature, poetry and the like, but always for a specific purpose and that purpose had direct and manifest connection with Jehovah's relation to His people, as His people, while what are called the "inspirations" of genius may be used for any, even the most general purposes. Lastly; it was shown that the prophetic gift was not in the power of the prophet himself. He could not make an appointment to prophesy on a certain Sunday morning, as we appoint to preach. It was not an ever-available faculty; It came and went as God chose. A prophet could no more prophesy of himself than an organ could utter passages of music of itself. The prophet might make mistaken inferences from his own inspired message. The Dr. gave some of these examples from Scripture.

But all men have a spiritual capability of seeing quite distinct from the bodily. There is an inner sight. That may be cultivated just as much as the bodily organ, and should be. When cultivated, it has sometimes gone into ecstasy, in which men have seen what could never be represented, and heard, as Paul did, would not be possible to be translated into any human language. Perhaps some such state was that into which the young man after Elisha's prayer; or it may be developed by holy living and deep and constant communion with God, more or less, the vision of God; and the daily effort of our lives should be to reach this state. The preacher here employed the phrase not as meaning a sight of God, but a sight of things generally as they appear to God—the man getting more nearly to God's standpoint, that is " the vision of God."

Elisha did not pray for the king, mark—but for the young man. And what did he pray for? More angels, a larger encampment of God's cohorts around the men who were his servants? No. He prayed for more sight. That is what is needed. We need not a single additional atom of matter or impulse of force in the universe for our science. All we need is more scientific insight. The world of Plato and the world of Bacon were the same, but a better insight has made in Greece, in England, and in the world, a greater conquest of nature to the uses and comfort of man. We need nothing more in the spiritual world, no additional revelation, but we need more spiritual insight. When men have both these as largely as God wills, we shall have a world whose glories will transcend all the golden dreams of poets.

See what it did for this young man. First, it dispelled his fears. Here the preacher described the terrible influence of fear upon individuals and communities, and painted the picture of a society from which all fear had been cast out. Then there came an increase of faith. The real nature of faith as a rational conviction of the existence of facts, and the effects of this faith as an increase of human power, were presented. The result was the production of sure-comfort in the young man. For young men a light of the spiritual world was necessary.

1. To make them profound students. Without faith, no science. Little faith, superficiality. We must get below phenomena. Physical science is lower than intellectual science, physics inferior to metaphysics. Behind all is spirit. The scientific man whose eyes have never been opened to the spiritual world is a mere hewer of wood and drawer of water, a mere recorder of appearances, very little better than a thermometer or weather-vane.

2. It is necessary to enable him to correct false impressions made to the sight. Helmholz tells us that no man ever sees what he thinks he sees, speaking of the bodily organ of vision. How true, nay, truer, of the inner sight! Napoleon said Providence was always on the side of the heaviest artillery. If he had had an Elisha to pray for him, he might have seen that the really heaviest artillery is always on God's side, the side of right. The world is full of large men and large things that are not great, and great men and great things that are not large.

3. To enable them to resist temptation by seeing through the

devil. Heine says he called the devil, and when he came he was not ugly, he was not lame; he was the charming, lovable man whom he met at the Spanish ambassador's. The devil is not always a man. You may call the devil at Saratoga, in New York, in highest London society, and *she* will come; and she will be as fresh as the spring, as warm as the summer, and sweeter than all deliciousness. But, all the same, she is the very devil. Blessed is the young man who sees the fiend in the appearance, as the Apostle says, of an angel of light.

Lastly, young men, to win, to touch the top of manhood, to be brought off more than conquerors, must always cast themselves on the side of the right. That is not always the side of numbers, rank, position, power and social distinction. The right does not always carry the promise of victory on its brow. Young men must take the right side when it is in the smallest minority, even if they feel assured that it may never attain to majority in their lifetime. That they may have the courage of their convictions, they must have their eyes open, that like the young man Moses, they may walk as seeing Him that is invisible, and so endure.

In conclusion, young men were urged to associate with good older men, and the old men to pray especially for the young that their eyes may be opened. Dr. Deems spoke rejoicingly of the success of the Young People's Societies of Christian Endeavor, of the good done by that in the Church of the Strangers, and urged all churches and pastors to nourish them, not only for the benefit of the young men themselves, but for the good of the churches. He believed that the new movement marked an epoch in the history of modern Christianity.

ADDRESS

BY DR. TWITCHELL, OF NEW HAVEN.

(*Reproduced from memory.*)

Mr. President and friends of the Society of Christian Endeavor: I am on my way with a friend to the Adirondack region on a fishing tour, but have stopped here for a day that I might look into the faces of this great gathering of Christian young men and women, who represent so many societies, and have convened here in council concerning the works of Christ. This, to me, is an especially inspiring assembly.

I am called upon very unexpectedly to address you; have had no time to arrange my thoughts, and can only speak to you out of the fullness of my heart, as thoughts shall crowd upon me, and words may be given.

I have attended many national religious conventions — several in this very church. I have seen this floor and these galleries crowded with representative pastors and laymen from all over the land, talking over the needs of this lost world, and planning for the spread of the gospel ; but I have never been more deeply impressed than I am at this very moment, facing as I do these hundreds who are counselling with each other, and praying together for greater power of usefulness in the vineyard of the Lord.

Mr. President, this gathering marks an epoch in the work of our churches. We are living in an age when Christian forces are multiplying, and marshalling in mighty volume for the conquest of the world for Christ. I should distrust my own personal relation to Jesus Christ, if my heart was not moved in an unwonted manner.   Eight hundred Societies of Christian Endeavor represented here on this floor — and these representing as many different local churches !

Last evening I overheard a conversation as I sat in one of these pews. A man, evidently a minister, (you know the profession is not always concealed) came down the aisle, and, speaking to another just behind me, who was evidently also a clergyman, said, " Do you think that the Society of Christian Endeavor has in it the elements of permanence?" The friend addressed seemed to think it had, though he did not answer with very much of emphasis or assurance.

I am no prophet, nor the son of a prophet ; but I venture that the fifty thousand now composing this "Union Society," in five years will become *five hundred thousand;* and I would not be at all surprised, if, in ten years, it should roll up A ROUND MILLION. It is *Christian,* on the right basis, and breathes the true, prophetic, life. God has a place for it, and a work for it, and help for it, I am sure. Blessing shall attend it. How patriarchal our brother Clarke, the founder, will feel ten years hence, if he shall become the foster-father of a *million!*

The ways of God are wonderful. For every great need of His church and the world He has provision. Sometimes *men* are wanted ; they are found ; sometimes *associations;* they are formed,— in the place, at the time, and for the uses which call for them. A century ago the Sabbath-school had birth. What marvels have been wrought by it! Now, societies of Christian endeavor; what good has already been accomplished by them! And the end is not yet.

Great changes have come over the convictions and customs of the churches in the last half-century. Time was when child conversion was distrusted, and when few children were admitted to the church. In many a church you could find scarcely one under sixteen or eighteen years of age. Now the children are welcomed and sought; they are found beautifully illustrating the faith of the Gospel, and they are more than welcome as church members. In some churches, those under twenty years of age constitute a large proportion. I, for one, rejoice in this changed condition of things. Not only the children, but pastors and churches, are to be congratulated. At what age a child may sincerely love and truly serve the Lord, I venture not to say ; but this I know — I have seen as lovely child-piety as adult-piety. I think that children often put us older people to shame with their consistency and Christian zeal. Time was also, and that within my memory, when few young people, though professing Christians, ever participated in social religious meetings. The minister would lecture, the deacons or elders pray, long metre hymns would be sung, the meeting called "opened," when it was fearfully *shut*, and the benediction pronounced. There was no encouragement for testimony, none for exhortation. The young people did not feel at home in the meetings of the church, and consequently few of them attended. Seldom, if ever, was a young man of eighteen or twenty called upon to pray ; and as for young women's speaking, that was never heard of !

How times have changed ! Now the voices of young men and women are welcome in church meetings ; their testimony sought. They come and speak, they constitute the warm life-blood of our churches. They are lifted into office, given work to do and are beco.ning grandly influential. The consequence is that our churches are beginning to be wide-awake and aggressive. I am here instituting no comparisons between the worth of the experience and counsel of age, and the fervor of youth. But this I affirm, the infusion of this youthful element into the worship and work of the churches, in some cases, has been like life from the dead. And the organization of these Societies of Christian Endeavor has had much to do in bringing this about. The young people have wanted something to do ; they have found something to do, and they are learning to do it. As was said a few moments ago by the speaker who preceded me, "Christian living is an art." Young Christians are learning this art in their weekly meetings. Christian usefulness is also an art. They are learning this. The language of prayer has to be learned, and it never is learned until we exercise ourselves in vocal prayer. The same of Christian address. We come to be able to bear testimony by testifying. We learn how to express the truth by expressing it ; how to exhort by exhorting. Scores and hundreds of young men, through the influence of these societies, are being trained up for efficiency in the Lord's vineyard.

It comes over me sometimes that this generation of preachers and teachers, and office-bearers in the church will soon have served their time. Pulpits and chairs of Sabbath school superintendents and teachers will change hands. The venerable secretaries of our great national Christian organizations will lay down their sacred trusts, and others will take them up. Who shall fill their places ? Preachers of the gospel are to come out of these societies ; missionaries among the heathen ; men and women who shall control the home and foreign work of the churches of this land. Three times every century these changes are made. God had the future in his thought when, down in Portland; Me., he moved his servant out upon this line. The preacher did not dream of what was being inaugurated. It was a small beginning. The growth has been grand. More is to follow.

The one special thought which I would leave with you, dear young friends, is *personal work*. *You* can reach the young as those older cannot. You are to seek them one by one, tell them what Christ has done for you ; tenderly invite them to try your Saviour, and join you in work for others.   God always goes before His servants as they go in search of souls, and always prepares the way.   (*Here numerous illustrations were given of the blessed results of personal labor.*)

It is enough to be under the direction of the enlightening and guiding spirit.   Count the cost of the service of Christ, young friends; but count no sacrifice too great if you may win souls.   May God bless you as you go down from this holy mount, and make you a blessing to many in the year to come.   No honest work for the Master is ever done in vain.   The seed may be long in sprouting, and the harvest long in ripening;   but both are sure, and the reward shall be great.   "Harvest Home" by and by shall be sung;   and then what joy!   Yield to no discouragement;   falter in the face of no obstacle.   God and one anointed soul are more than a match for the world!

www.ingramcontent.com/pod-product-compliance
Lightning Source LLC
Chambersburg PA
CBHW020508040426
42331CB00042BA/97